AF229726

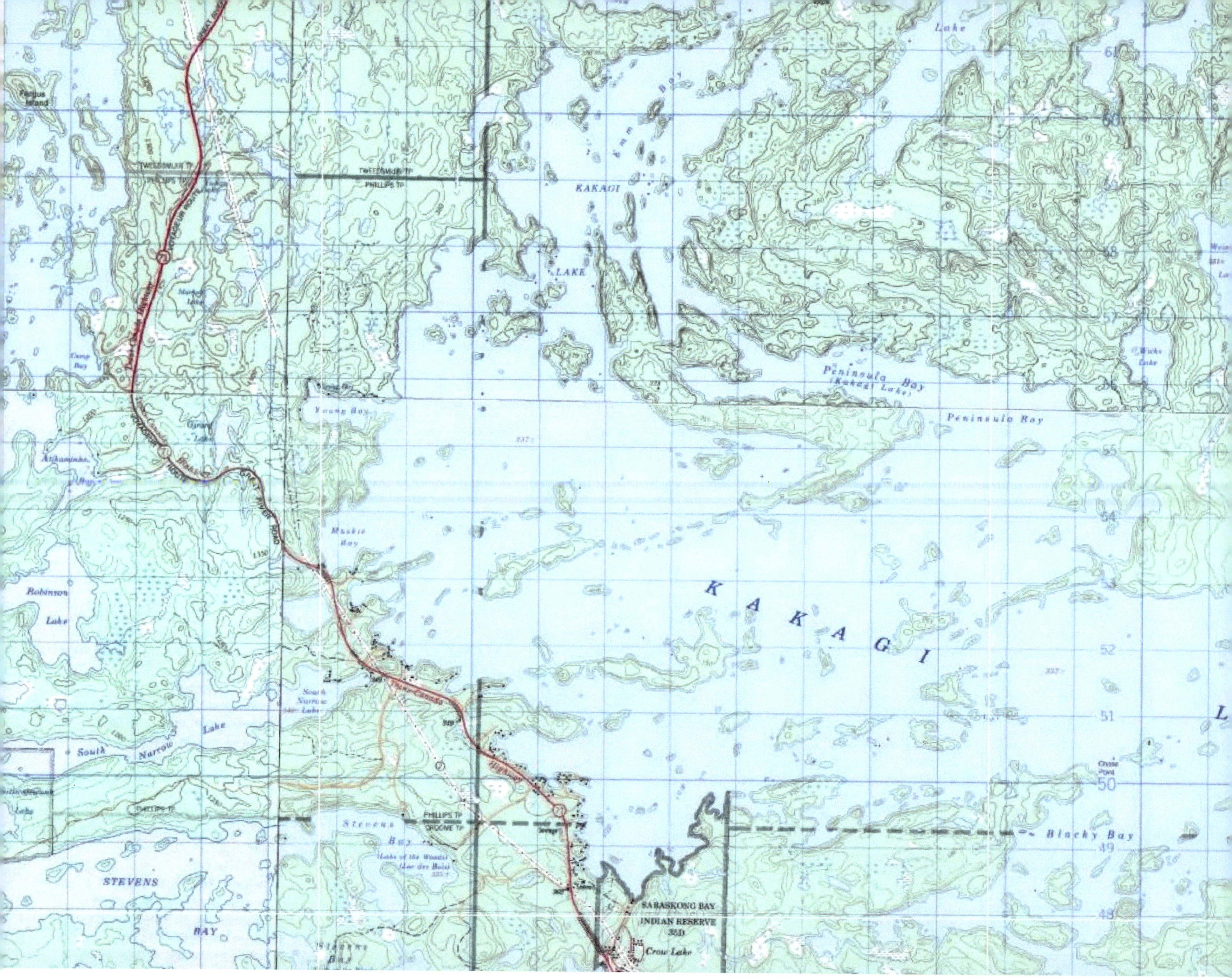

Fergus Island
TWEEDSMUIR TP
PHILLIPS TP
TWEEDSMUIR TP
PHILLIPS TP
KAKAGI
LAKE
Camp Bay
Muskeg Lake
Grassy Lake
Atikaminka Bay
Young Bay
Peninsula Bay (Kakagi Lake)
Peninsula Bay
Wicks Lake
Lake
Muskie Bay
Robinson Lake
South Narrow Lake
K A K A G I
L
South Narrow Lake
Crane Pond
STEVENS
PHILLIPS TP
PHILLIPS TP
GROOME TP
Stevens Bay
Swamp
Blacky Bay
Lake of the Woods (Lac des Bois)
SARASKONG BAY INDIAN RESERVE 35D
BAY
Bay
Crow Lake

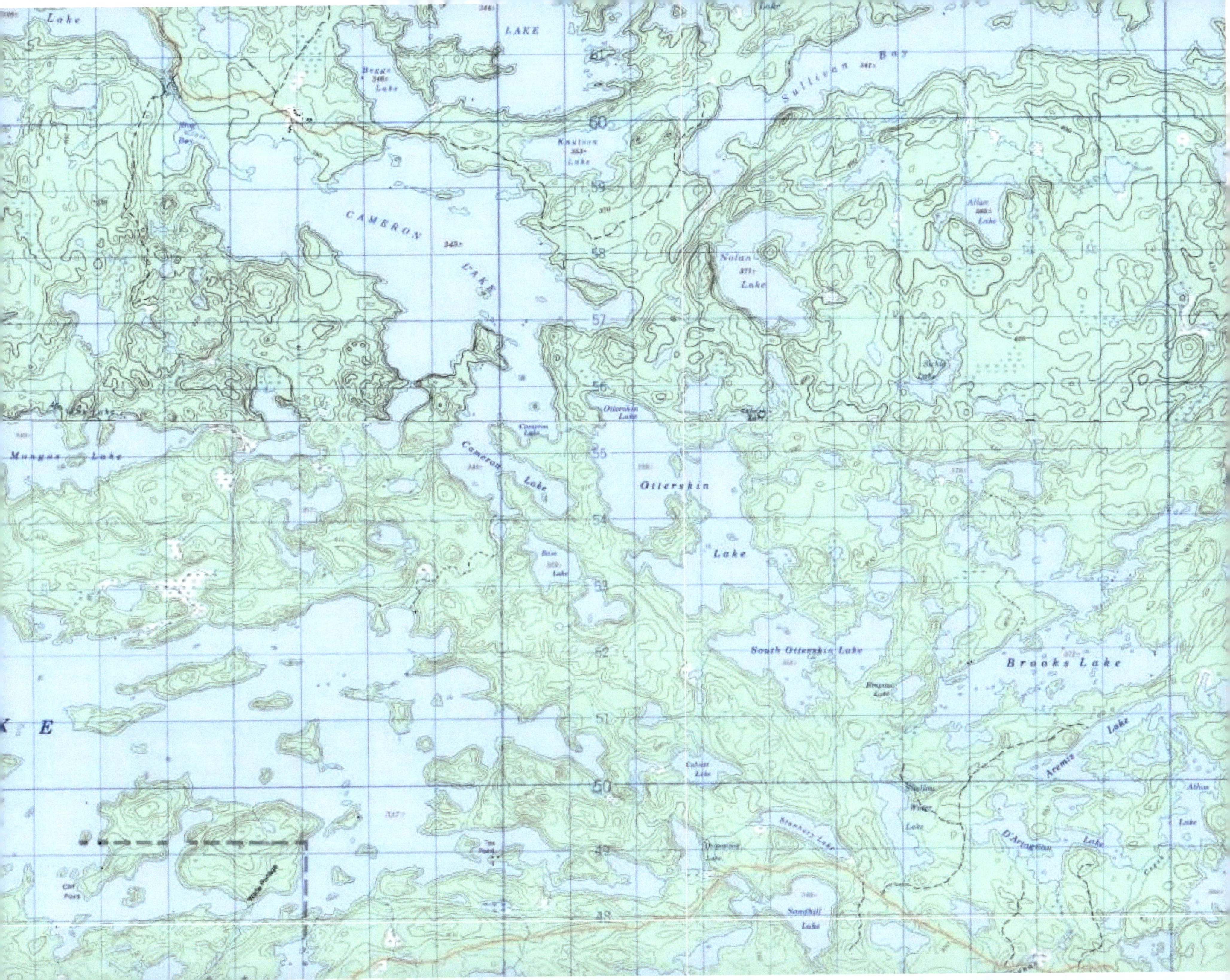

Lake
LAKE
Sullivan Bay
Beggs Lake
Knutson Lake
Allen Lake
CAMERON LAKE
Nolan Lake
Otterskin Lake
Cameron Lake
Mungus Lake
Otterskin
Lake
Bass Lake
South Otterskin Lake
Brooks Lake
Aramis Lake
Athos Lake
Cabot Lake
D'Artagnan Lake
Stanbury Lake
Sandhill Lake
Cliff Point

PARADISE NORTH

William D. Van Atta Jr.

A Collection Of Poems, Writings, and Photographs

Contents

Dedication

To my mom, dad, three brothers and three sisters for all their loving support over the years. To the many precious furry and winged companions, I have had the honor of experiencing life with.

Acknowledgment

I would like to give special thanks to my mom who introduced me to the poems of her grandfather, Joseph Russell Taylor and his acquaintance, Robert W. Service. Thank you to the many teachers who patiently helped me with my deficient reading and writing skills. For introducing me to north woods I would like to thank the Whiteway's, Dr. Robert (Red) and wife Marion. I worked my way through college as the Whiteway's handy man.

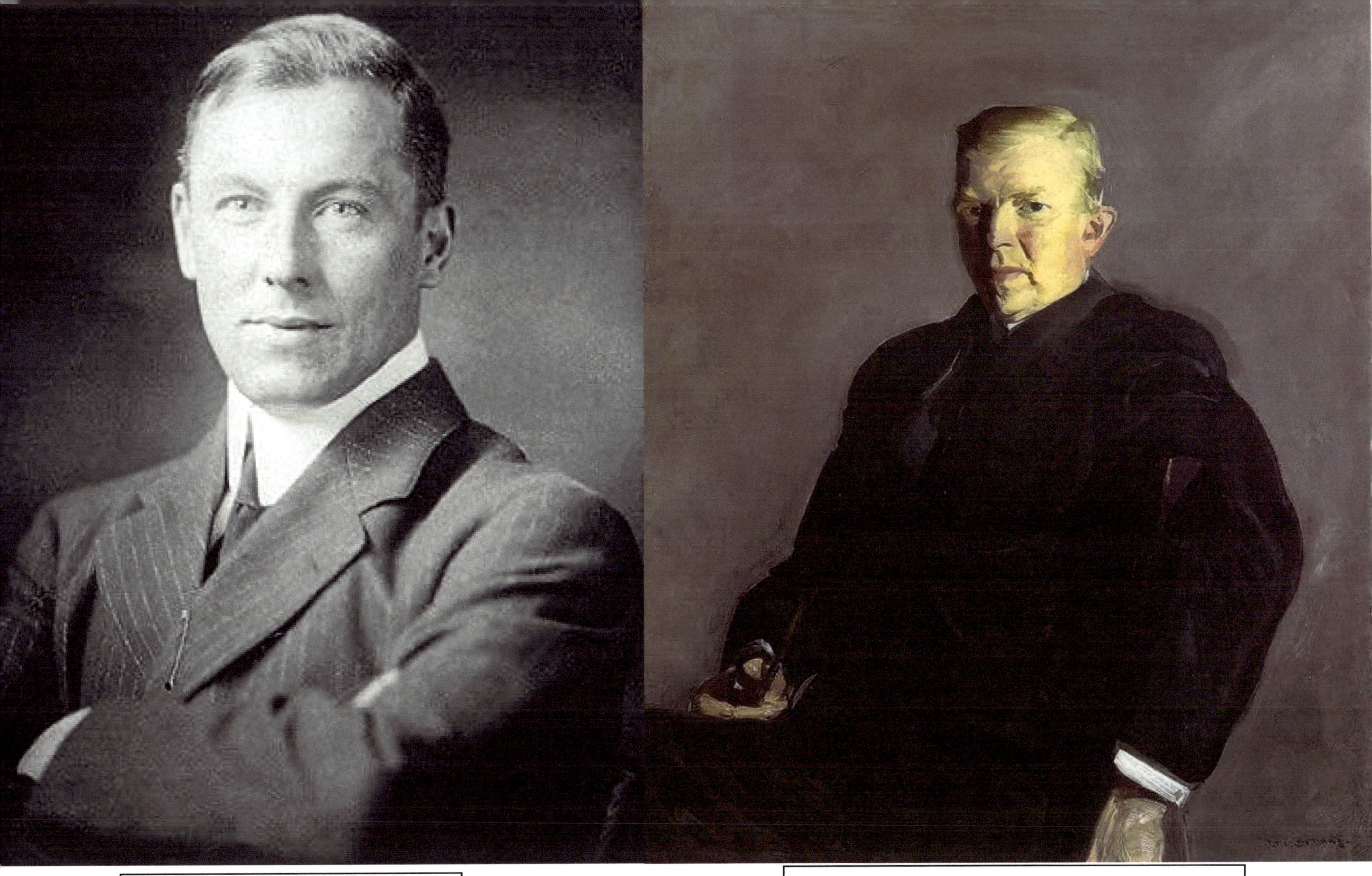

Robert W. Service

Professor Joseph Russell Taylor
Portrait by George Bellows

About the Author

William (Bill) D. Van Atta Jr is a veteran Army aviator and retired registered nurse who is a native of the midwest, now living in La Crescent, Minnesota. Bill holds a Bachelor of Science degree in geography from the University of Wisconsin La Crosse. After 12 years of service in the U.S. Army as both a rotary wing and fixed wing aviator, Bill went back to school. He graduated from The Norfolk General Hospital School of Nursing and then competed his Bachelor of Science of Nursing degree at Excelsior University and was licensed as an RN. Bill practiced in several hospitals which included Level 1 and 2 Trauma Centers where he specialized in the care of surgical, trauma and burn patients. When not writing Bill enjoys spending time with his dogs. He especially likes being outdoors camping, hiking, and photographing nature. Over the past couple of years Bill has been putting his woodworking skills to test building a small sailboat. He is an avid swimmer and has competed in several open water swimming competitions. You can connect with Bill at: running_wolf57@yahoo.com

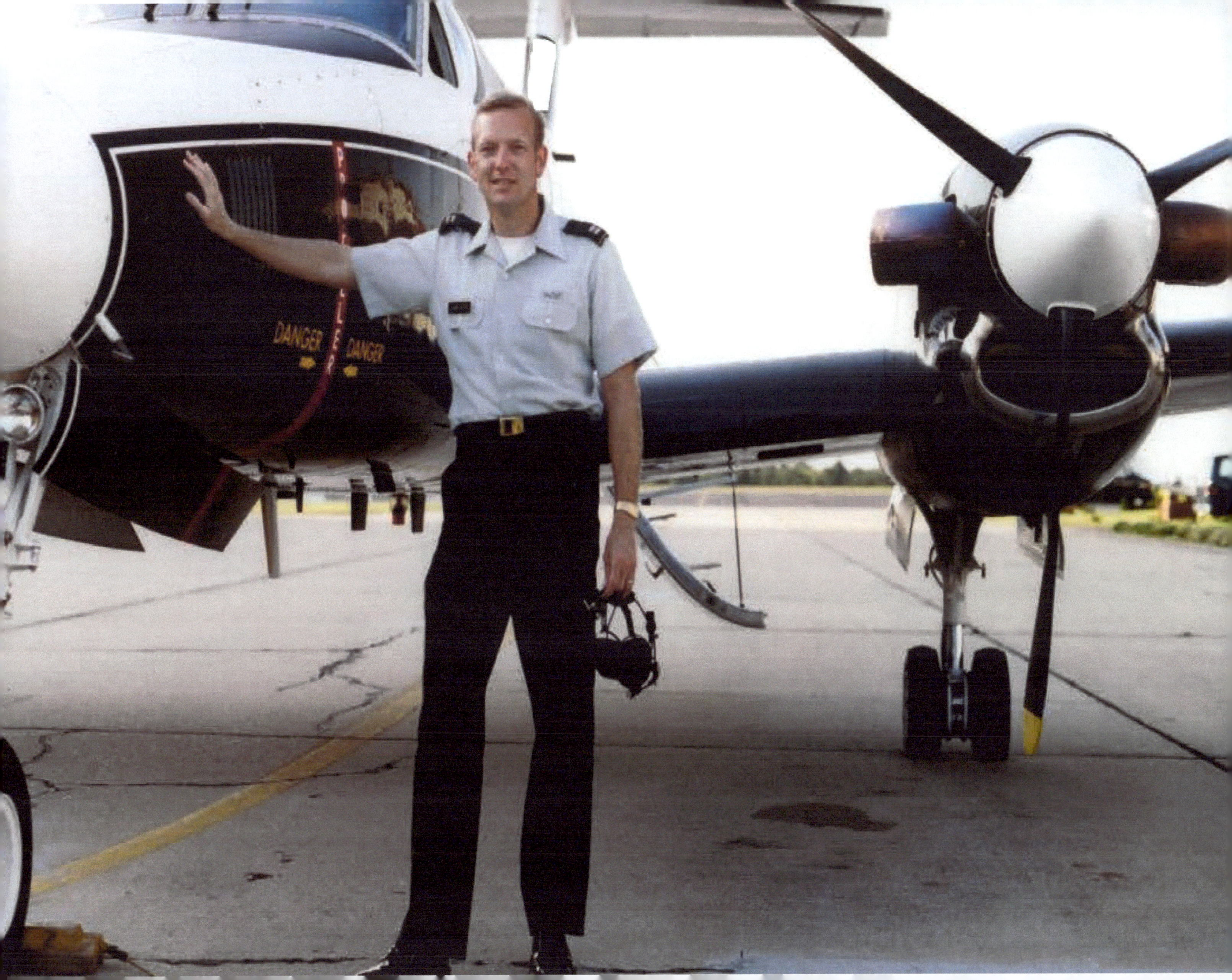

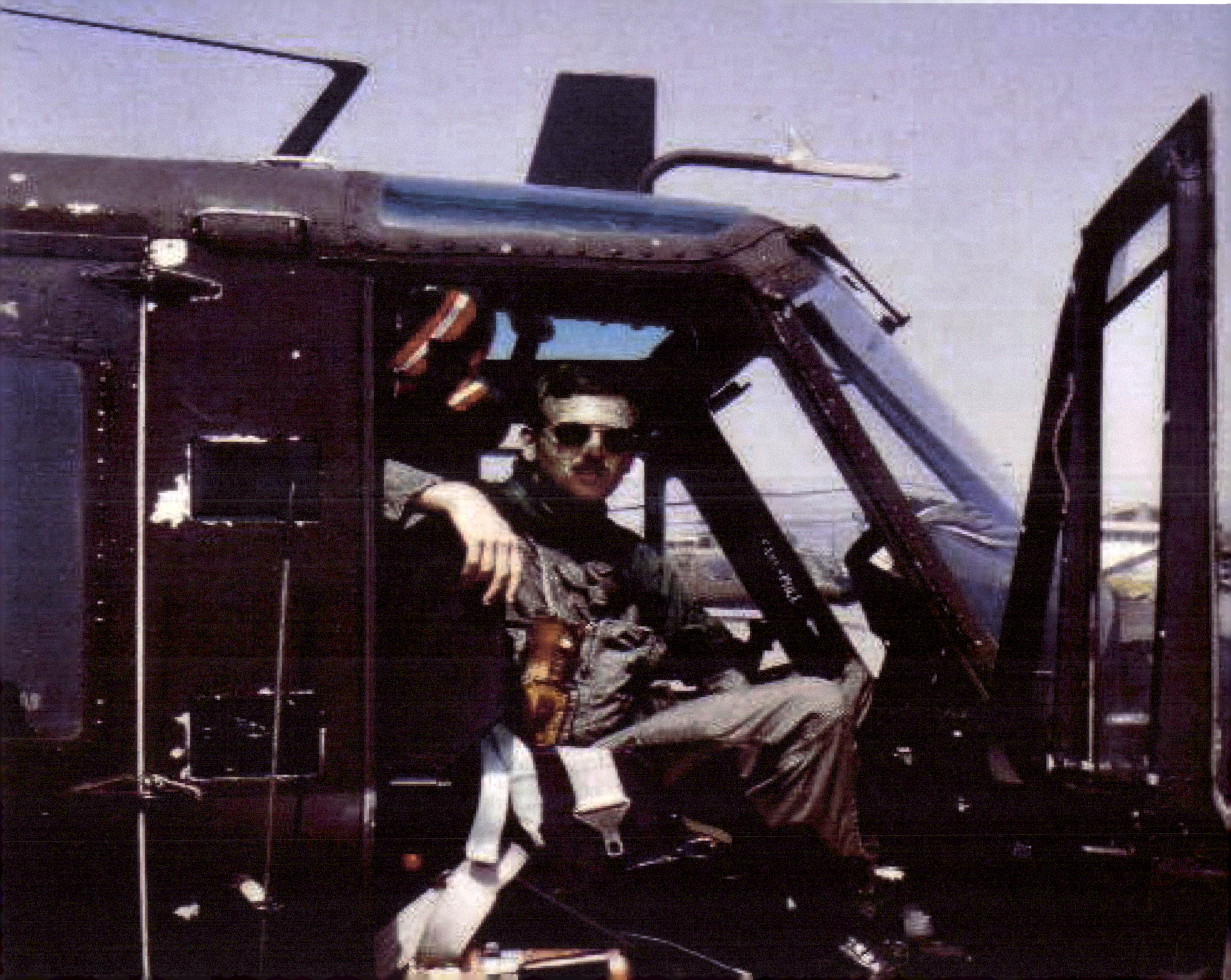

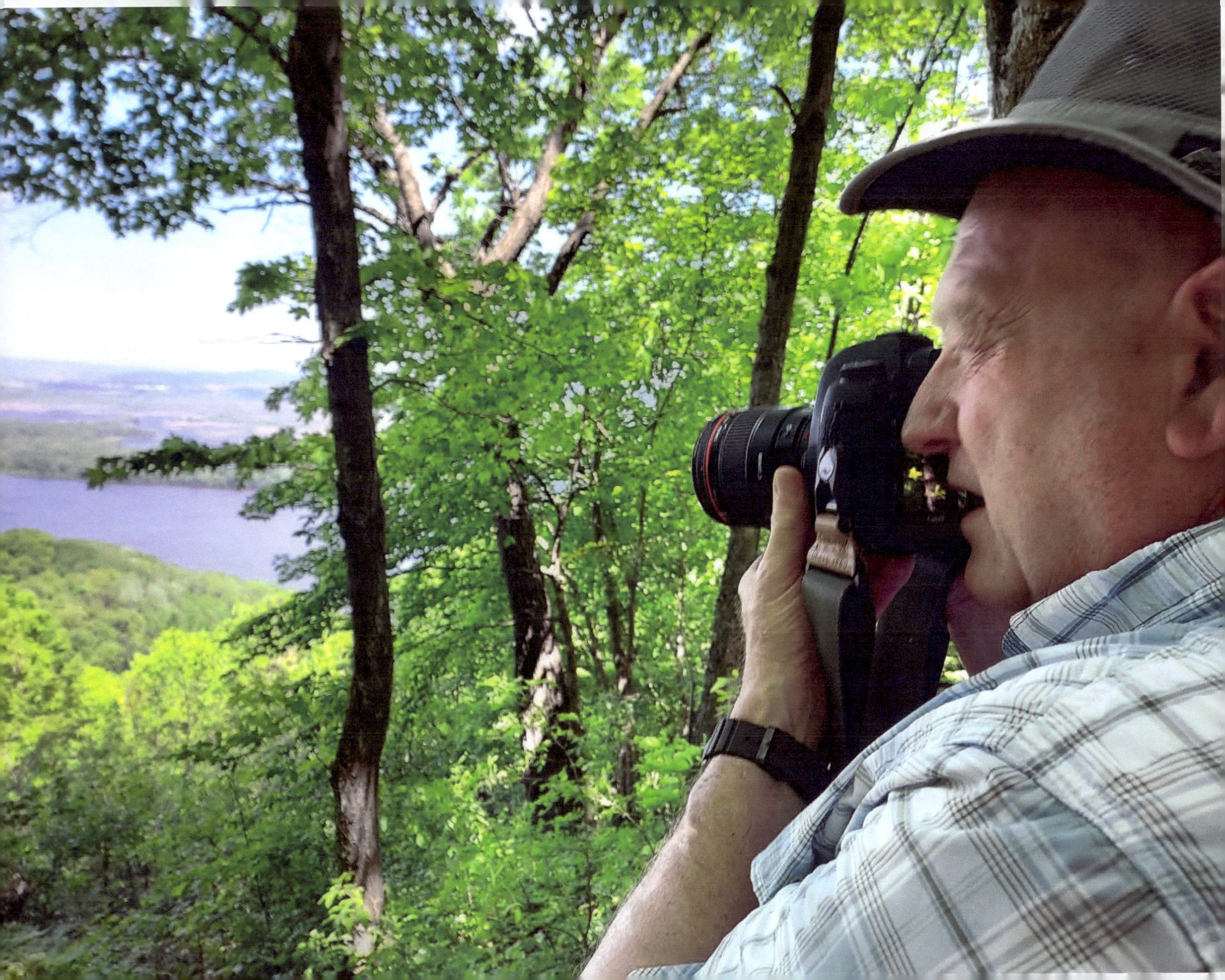

WINTER WIND

The wind, the wind, the wind it blows
It blows and blows, it blows so cold
It grasps you with its ice chilled hands
And carries you off to warmer lands
The wind, the wind, the wind it blows

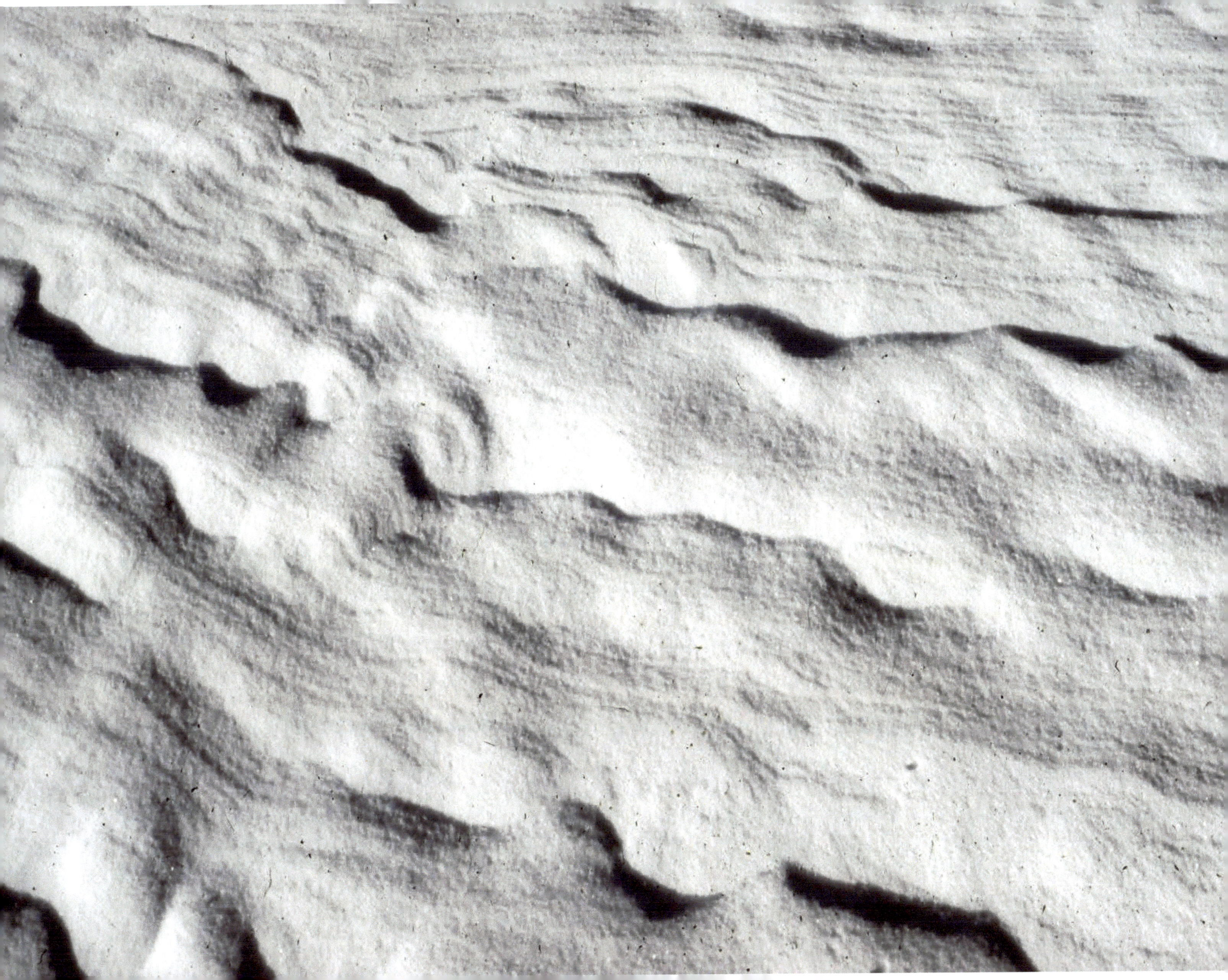

MY FRIEND

The wind is my friend, the wind it is.

It raps at my window, it knocks at my door,

It whistles and whines through the cracks in my floor.

And when the skies are clear and the nights are cold

It howls above the sounds of the fire's hot coals.

It is outside and I within, and the wind it tries to find its way in.

Shall I open my door and let it in?

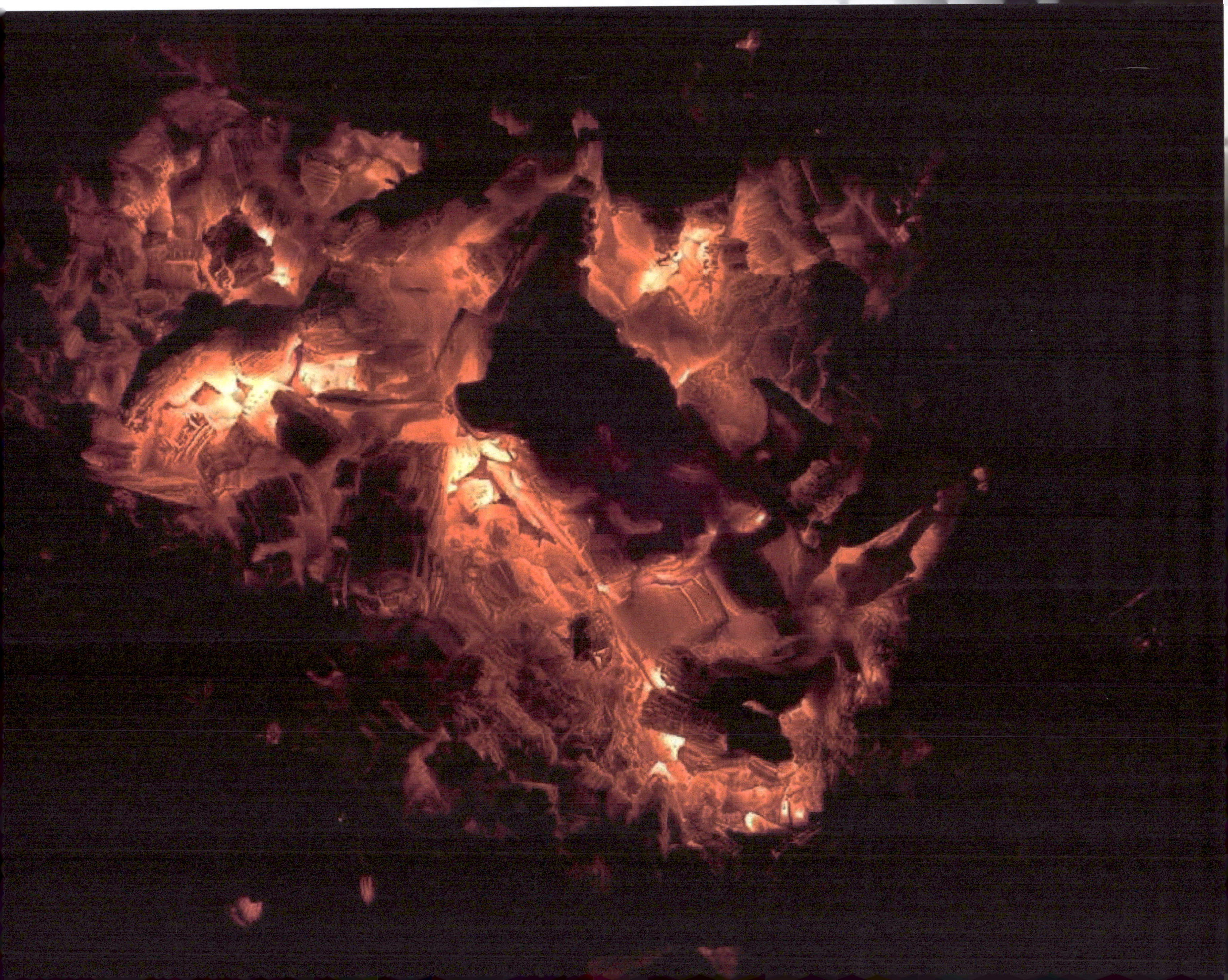

MARIAH'S SONG

Oh sweet Mariah, blaze a trail to a life far beyond this earth

To a paradise in the mountains where the streams run cool and pure Where gentle breezes blow in your face carrying enticing smells

And the sky, it's a cobalt blue with fluffy clouds of white

In the dark of night the stars and moon shine bright while the northern lights dance about

And there you'll howl those ancient tunes that echo through the night

As you run that trail look back for us, for we are not too far behind

But until then you'll run in our hearts where your memories are sacred, happy and dear

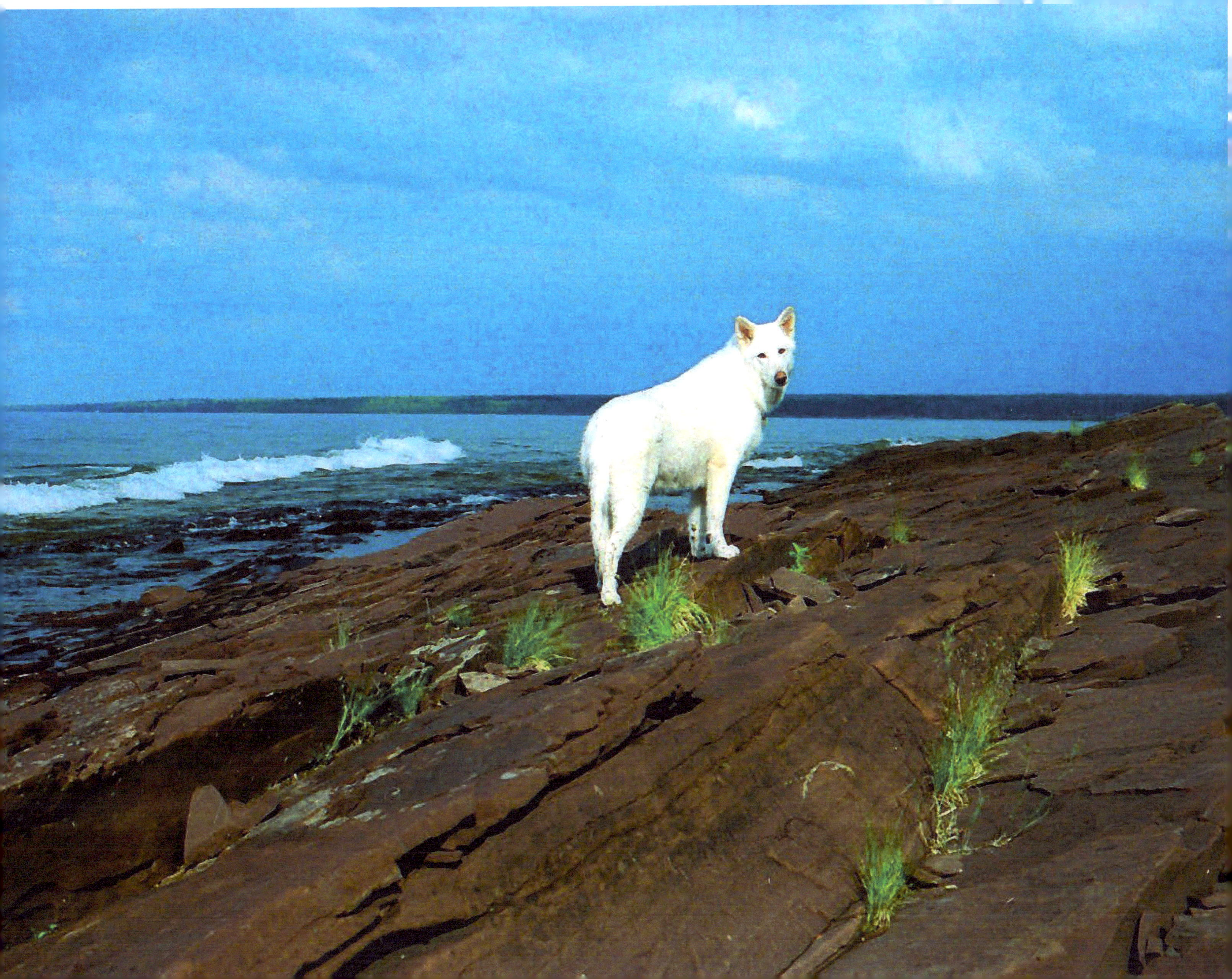

NIGHT FALL

The woods are quiet now

The wind it slowly dies

And the skies grow darker

Now giving way to the clearness of night

In the distance a loon can be heard

She sends her eeric cry across the glassy waters

To my shore nearby

And the sun

It releases its lasts rays

They dance and then die on the large pine trunks towering overhead

Then all, all is in darkness

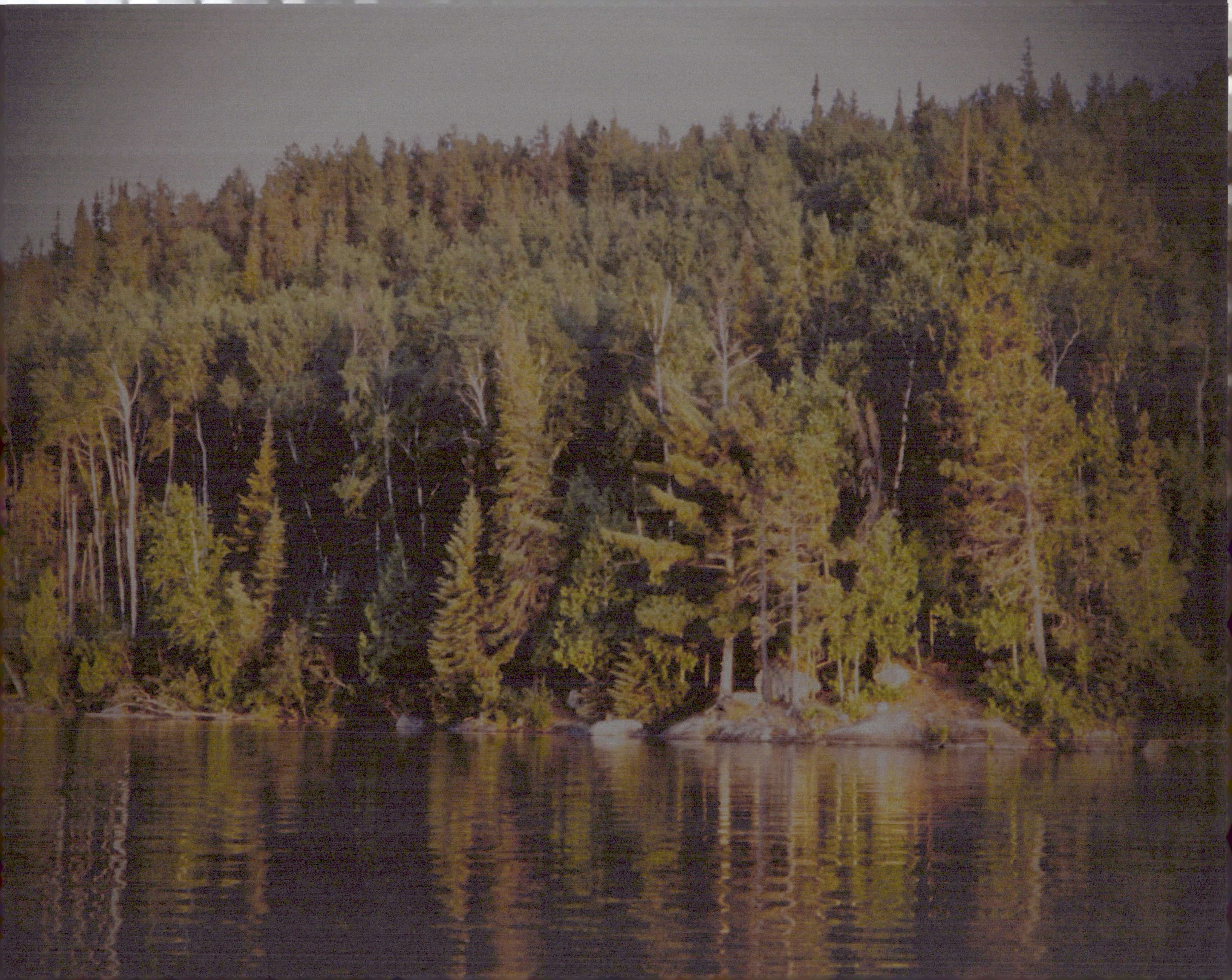

RIVERS

Rivers, rivers, rivers flow

Some are high and some are low

Some are fast and some are slow

In spite of all the things I know

I still am wondering

Where they go

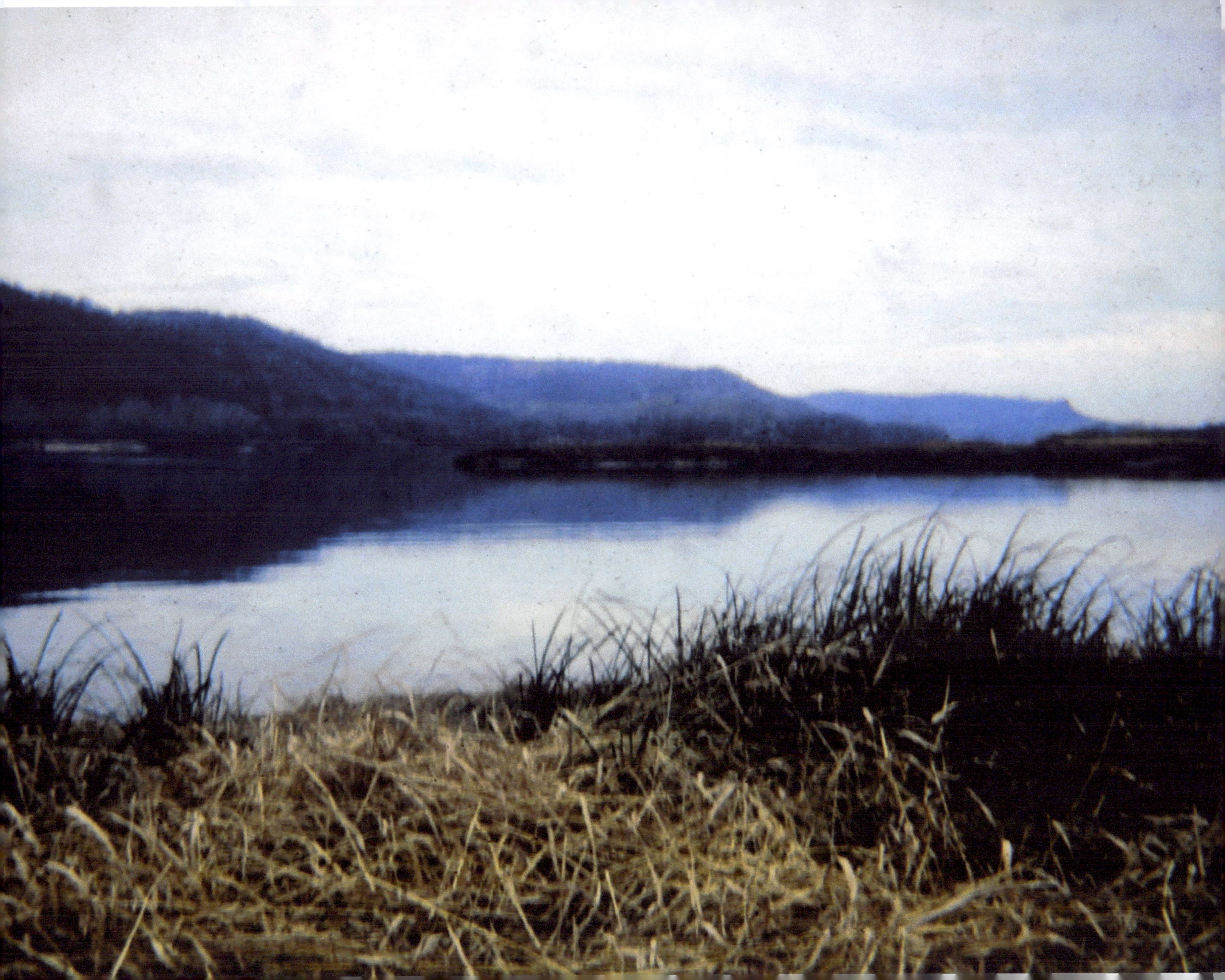

NORTHERN LIGHTS

The northern lights came out last night

Oh yes! And they greeted me

As I looked down on the mirrored lake

They looked up at me

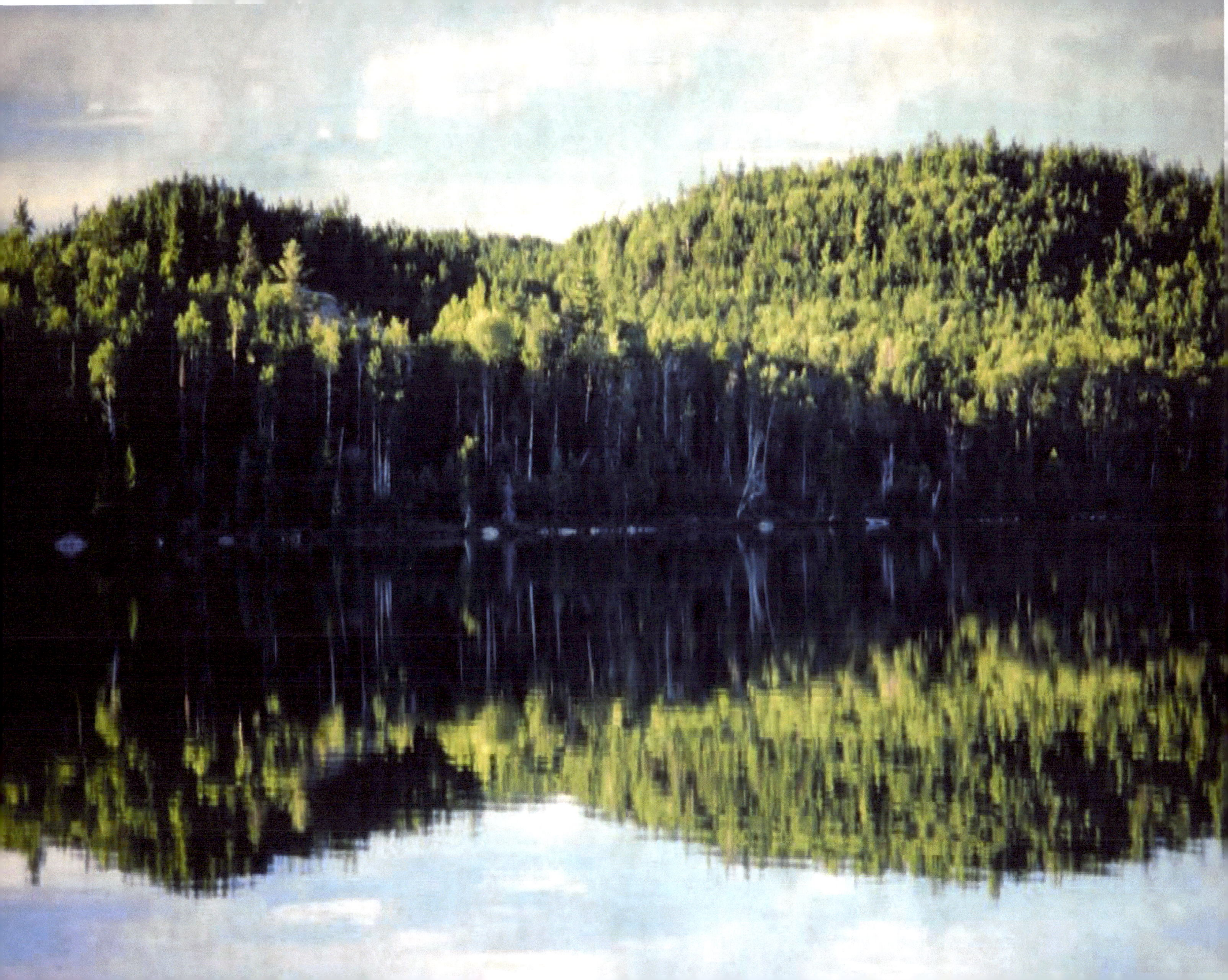

THE KAKAGI LAKE EXPRESS

It was a warm August day at Kakagi Lake in Ontario Canada, and we were looking for some relief and a treat. With a treat in mind, we made our way to the boat house and climbed aboard the small boat tied up to the dock. The boat, made of wood, appeared to be quite old. Its red hull was fading now from years of trusty use. It got its propulsion from a small Mercury outboard motor of 15 horsepower. I primed the motor, made a few pulls on the starter cord and the motor sputtered, then fired up, engulfing us in a white cloud of exhaust smoke and a smell of gasoline.

With a gentle twist on the throttle the boat lunged forward, and we began our journey across the lake. My sister Molly and I were on a mission. Our Task was to obtain a gallon of vanilla ice cream for the hot fudge sauce I would cook up for the evening dessert. We bounced about the boat as we entered the open water, navigating our way around numerous islands and carefully avoiding the rocky hazards that lay hidden below Kakagi's waves.

After 30 minutes of wind and spray we approached our destination. I throttled the motor back to a gentle rumble and coasted to the dock. We were now at Hanson's Hideaway Lodge. We strolled up the dock and up the hill to the lodge store. Entering the store, the squeaky screen door slammed shut behind us. At the counter we found Ellen Hanson. We greeted each other and talked a bit then made our way to the freezer. Molly opened the chest, reached through a frosty cloud, and pulled out a gallon of vanilla ice cream. We were on the clock now as we had to make it back before our icy treat completely melted.

With the carton secured in a styrofoam cooler and the bill paid we scrambled to the boat and headed back across the choppy lake. We were making good time on our ride to the Whiteway's Kakagi Wilderness Lodge, where my Mom, Dad, Molly, and I were guests, our hosts were Dr. (Red) and Mrs. (Marion) Whiteway.

The lodge, within viewing distance of the lake, was accessible only by boat and had been in Mrs. Whiteway's family since the 1930s. It had become forgotten and neglected over the years until it was brought to life again in the 1960s. There was no electricity or plumbing. Water was hauled in pails from the lake and bathing was done in Kakagi's frigid waters. It did however have the convenience of a propane fueled cooking stove and refrigerator/freezer.

We left the open waters, rounded an island and the green lodge and red boat house came into sight. I throttled back the motor and let the wind carry us to the dock. The sound of the trailing boat wake lapped along the rocky shore echoing through the air.

With the boat secured we headed up the trail to the lodge with our, hopefully, still frozen delight. We went inside to the waiting fridge and deposited the ice cream into the ice encrusted freezer compartment. With our mission successfully completed it was now time to make the chocolaty hot fudge sauce.

Where the recipe originated, I'm not sure. It was in my mom's recipe file on a three by five card that was stained with decades of spills from the recipe's ingredients. Already I had been cooking the sauce for years and the ingredients and cooking directions were burned into my memory. The hot fudge sauce, a mixture of butter, sugar, baker's chocolate, salt, vanilla extract, and evaporated milk was cooked to just below boiling. As it cooked a chocolaty aroma filled the kitchen air pushing against the smell of the towering pine forest outside.

Tonight, it was the guests turn to prepare the evening meal. I don't remember what my mom cooked up as it was so many years ago. I will however never forget the hot fudge sauce I made and poured over the dishes filled with vanilla ice cream.

Soon the dinner bell rang, and we all gathered around the long wood table in the lodge dining room enjoying company and the meal.

After a short break from dinner, we all took our seats again and dug into the sweet concoction placed before us. The only sound, spoons scooping up the delicious treat. With the treat complete, silence was replaced by conversation of memories past, joys of the present and adventures waiting in the future.

Night fall was fast approaching, the once blue sky, was now painted a pinkish red. It was time, time to light the Coleman lanterns. We lit the lanterns to a chorus of crying loons. The glowing lanterns' light filled the room and flickered on the rustic walls and moose head above the stone fireplace, bringing the old bull to life. The lanterns had a distinct hissing sound to them; it was a mesmerizing calming sound.

Well, it was getting quite late now, and we were all tired from the day's activities. Everyone said good night and I headed off to my room with lantern in hand. I placed my lantern on the table next to the bed and crawled between the flannel sheets. I reached over, turned the fuel knob to off and listened to the hissing subside. The light slowly faded as the lantern burned off the remaining fuel. It was now pitch black and I quickly fell asleep.

Even today with so many years past, I can hear the hiss of that lantern; see the glow of its light and taste that hot fudge over ice cream from the boat run called, the Kakagi Lake Express.

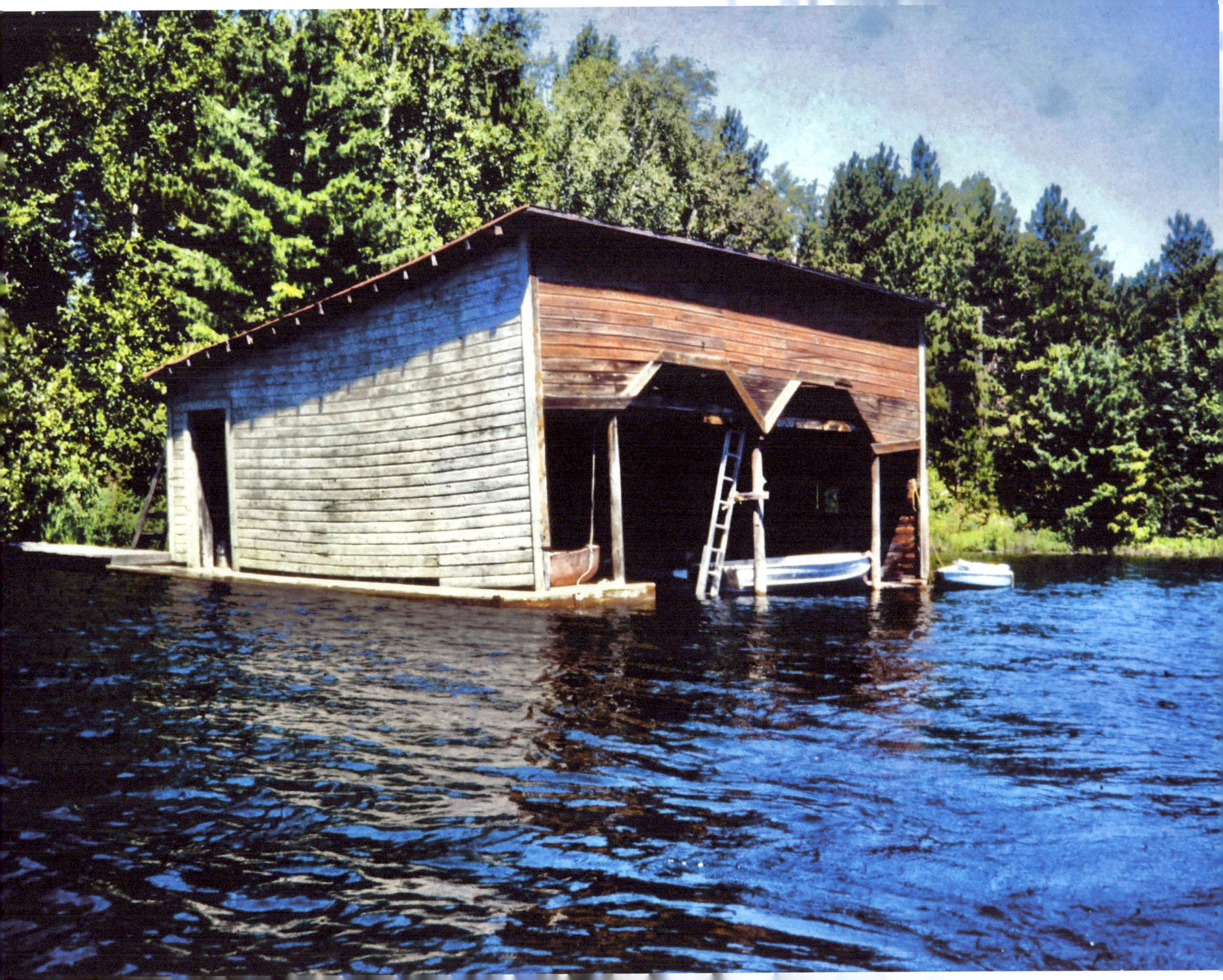

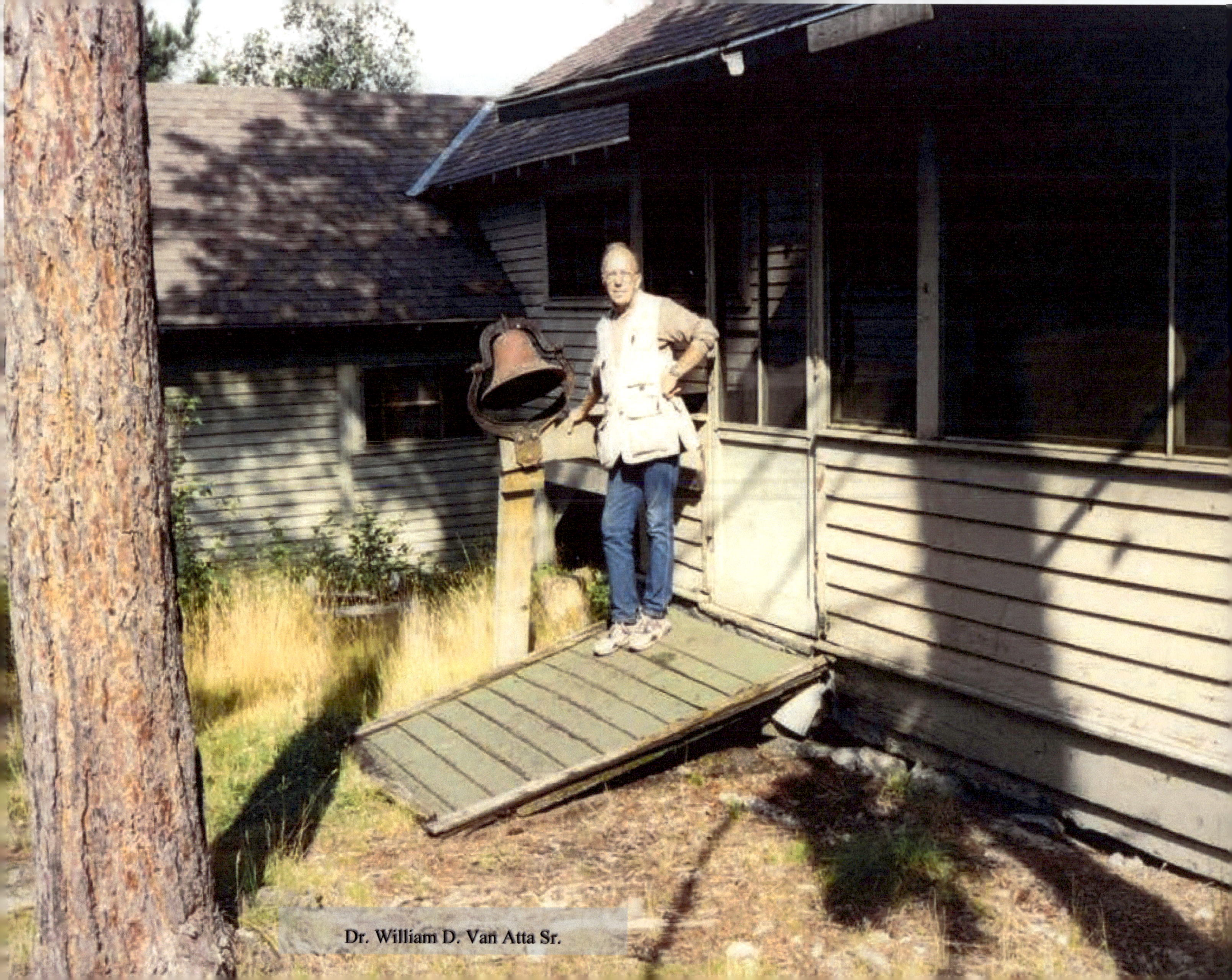

Dr. William D. Van Atta Sr.

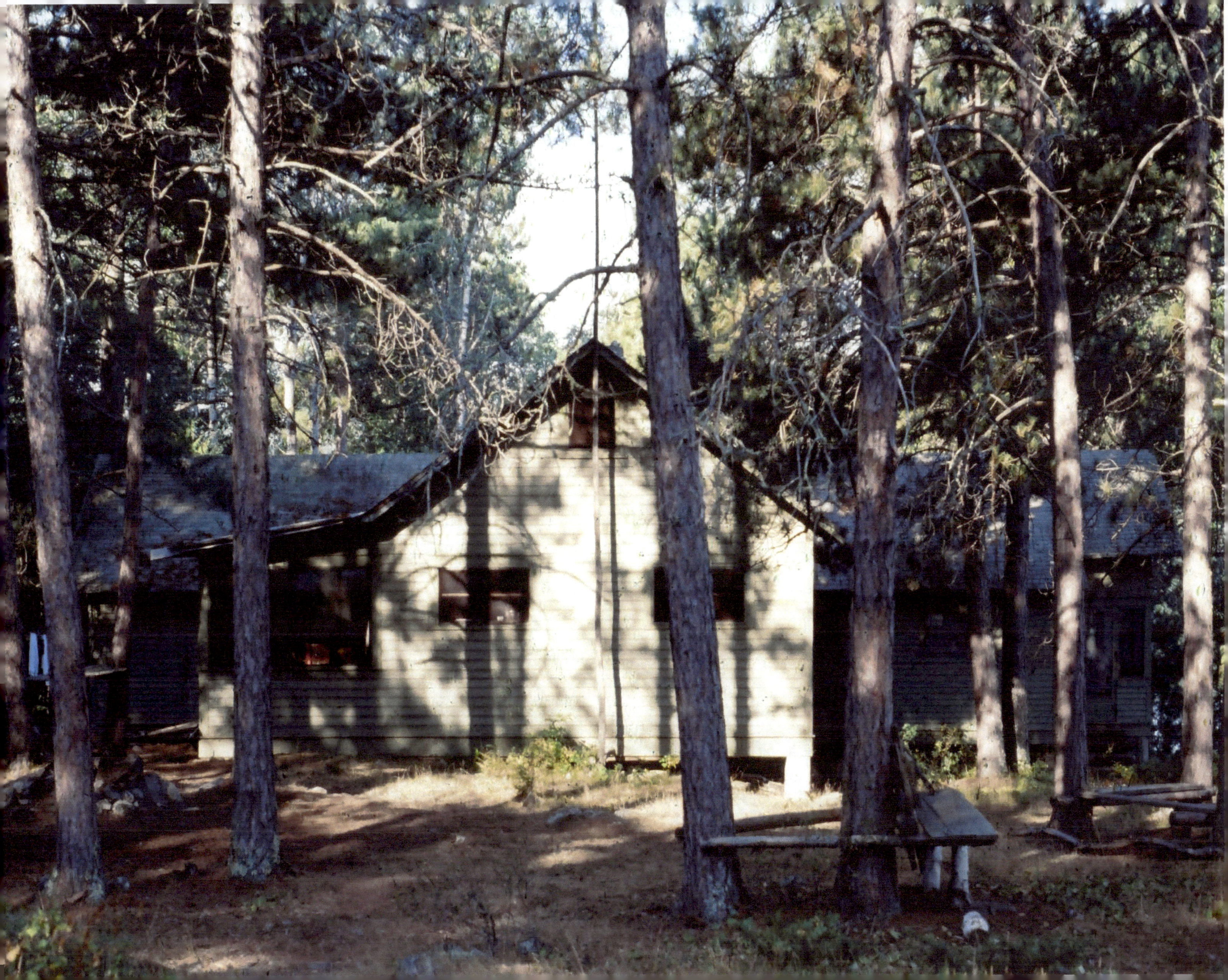

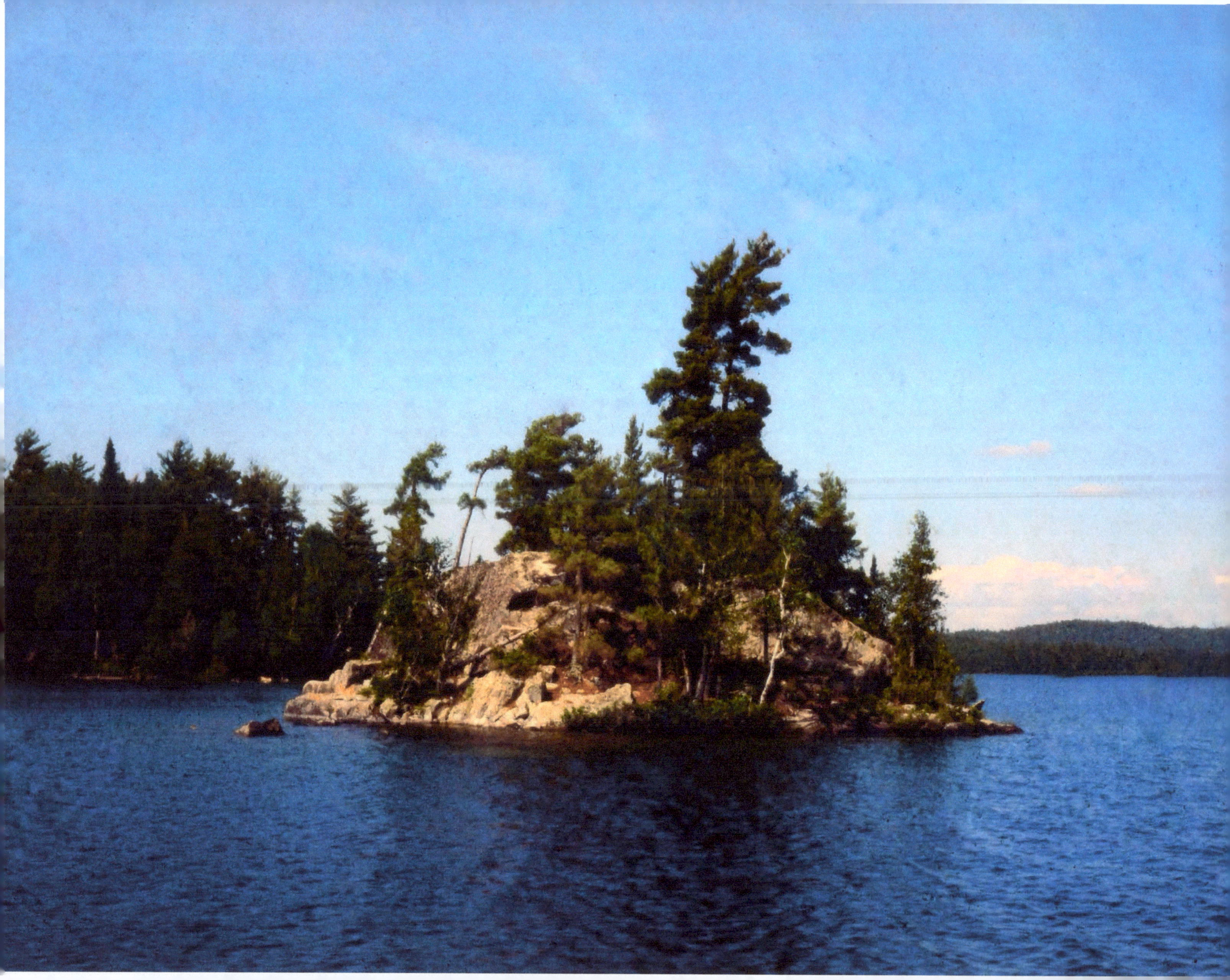

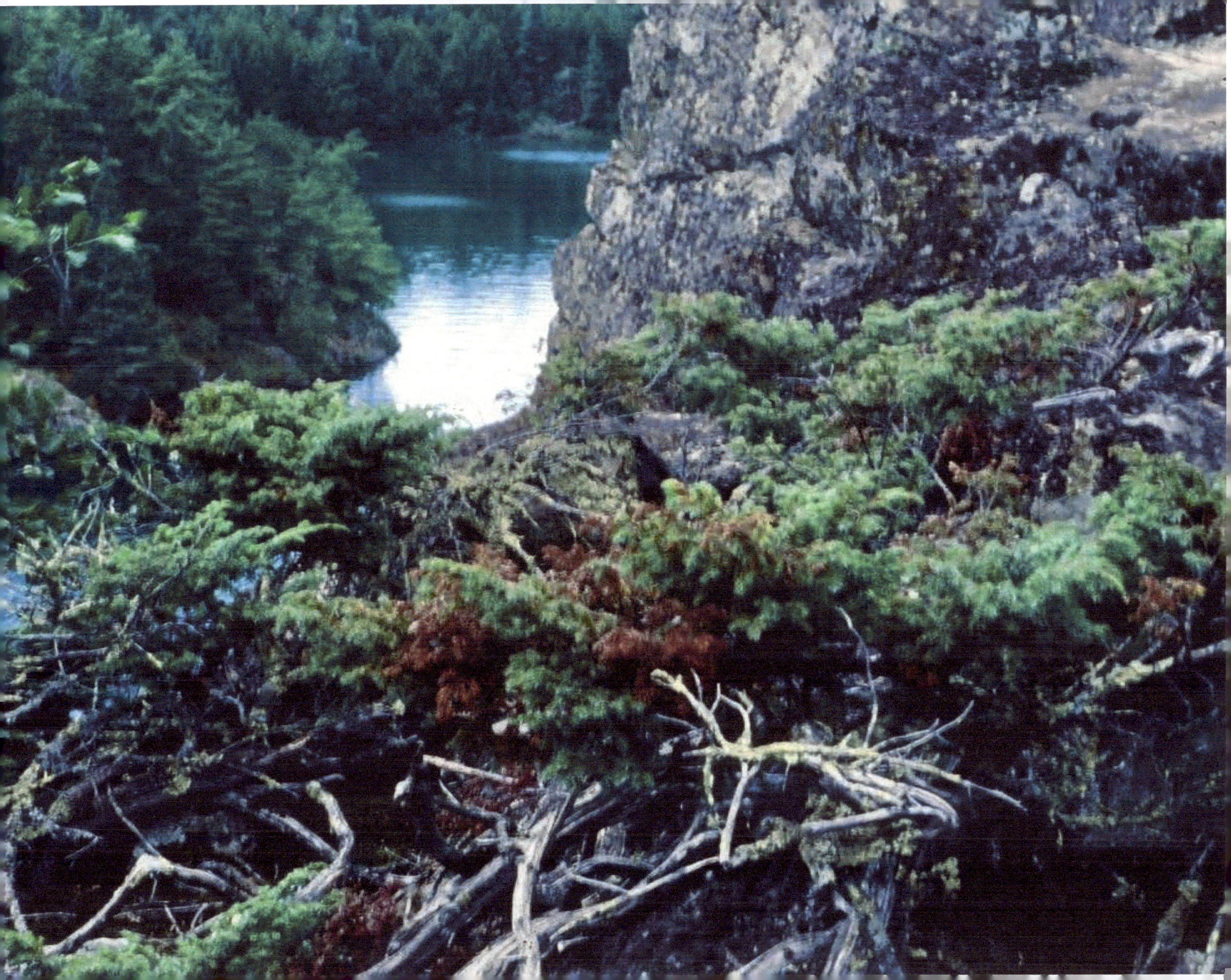

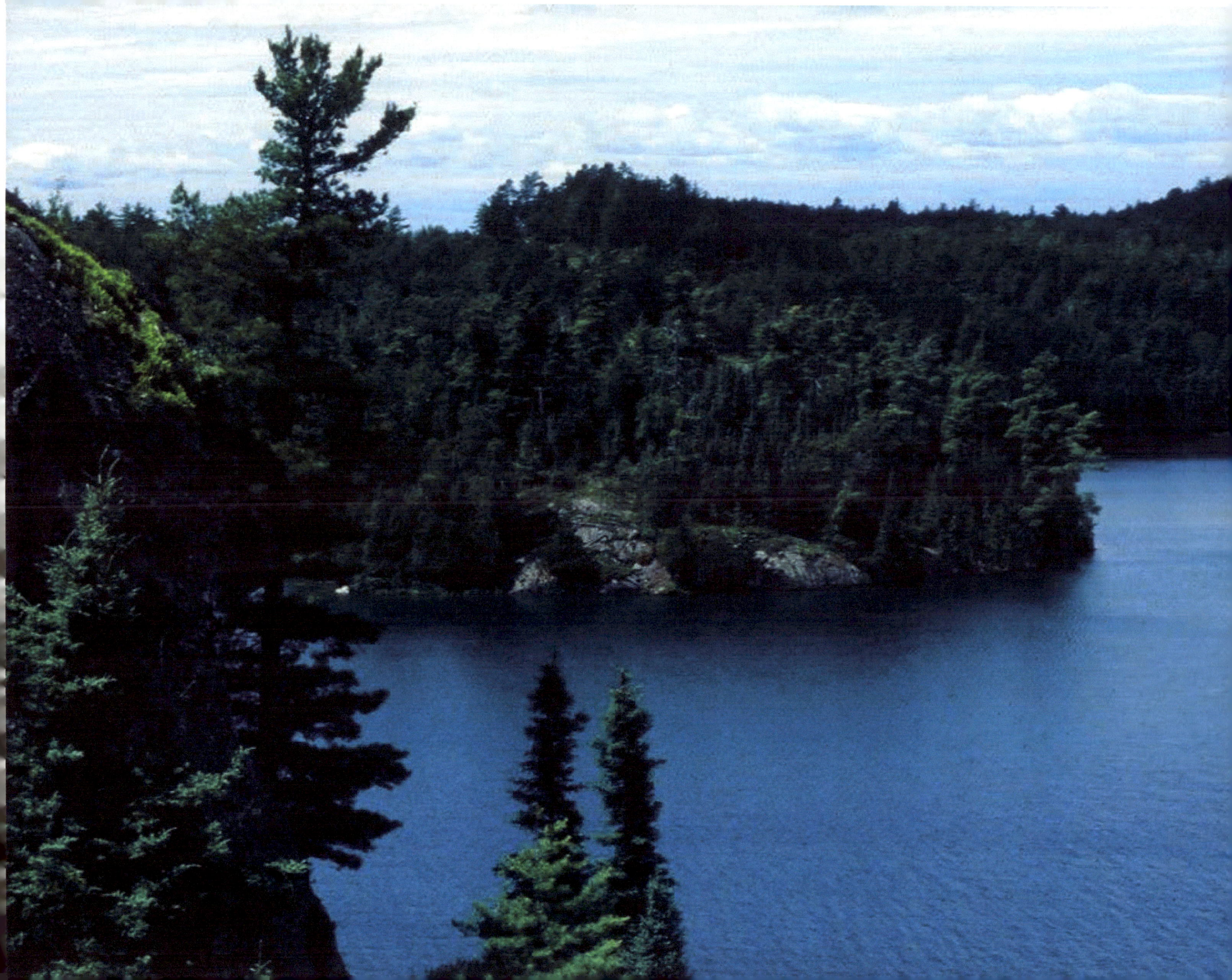

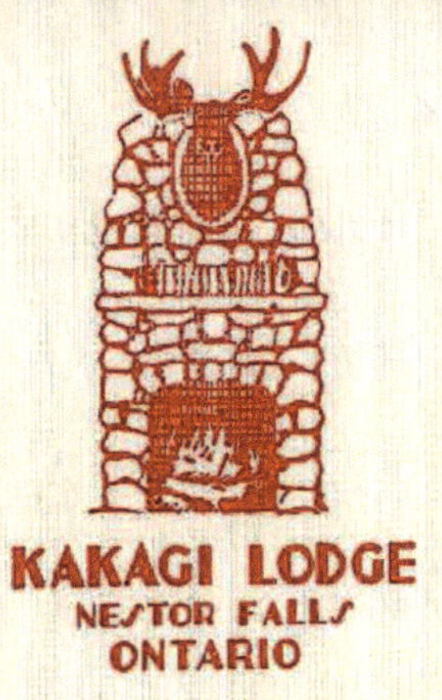

9/15/80

Dear Bill —
    We have decided to leave the lovely sunset photograph here at Kakagi — eventually to be in our cabin — Today is rainy and cold (45°) and The picture is a beautiful reminder of the long summer evenings —
    This is the latest we have ever been here and we certainly feel the Threshold of winter — as the aspen leaves are yellowing and falling and this years brown & dry needles cover the ground —
    Yesterday we heard & then saw the cranes high in the sky wheeling and organizing for their flight south — beautiful !!

We shall think of you often as you embark on a new phase of life — wishing you well all the way — Thank you for this photograph and the two others we have — and many other things I think you know —
        Sincerely —
        Marion & Dr. Whiteway

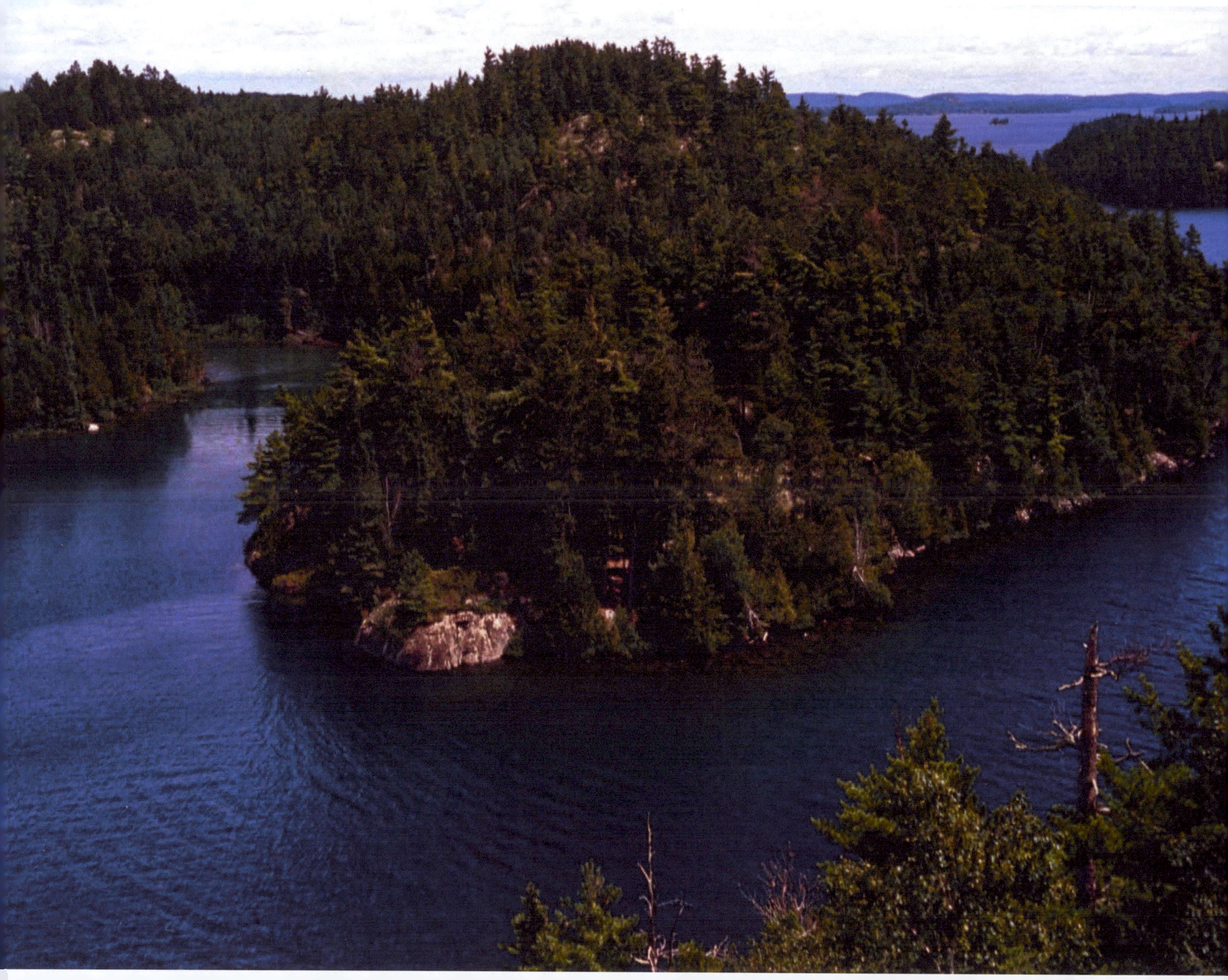

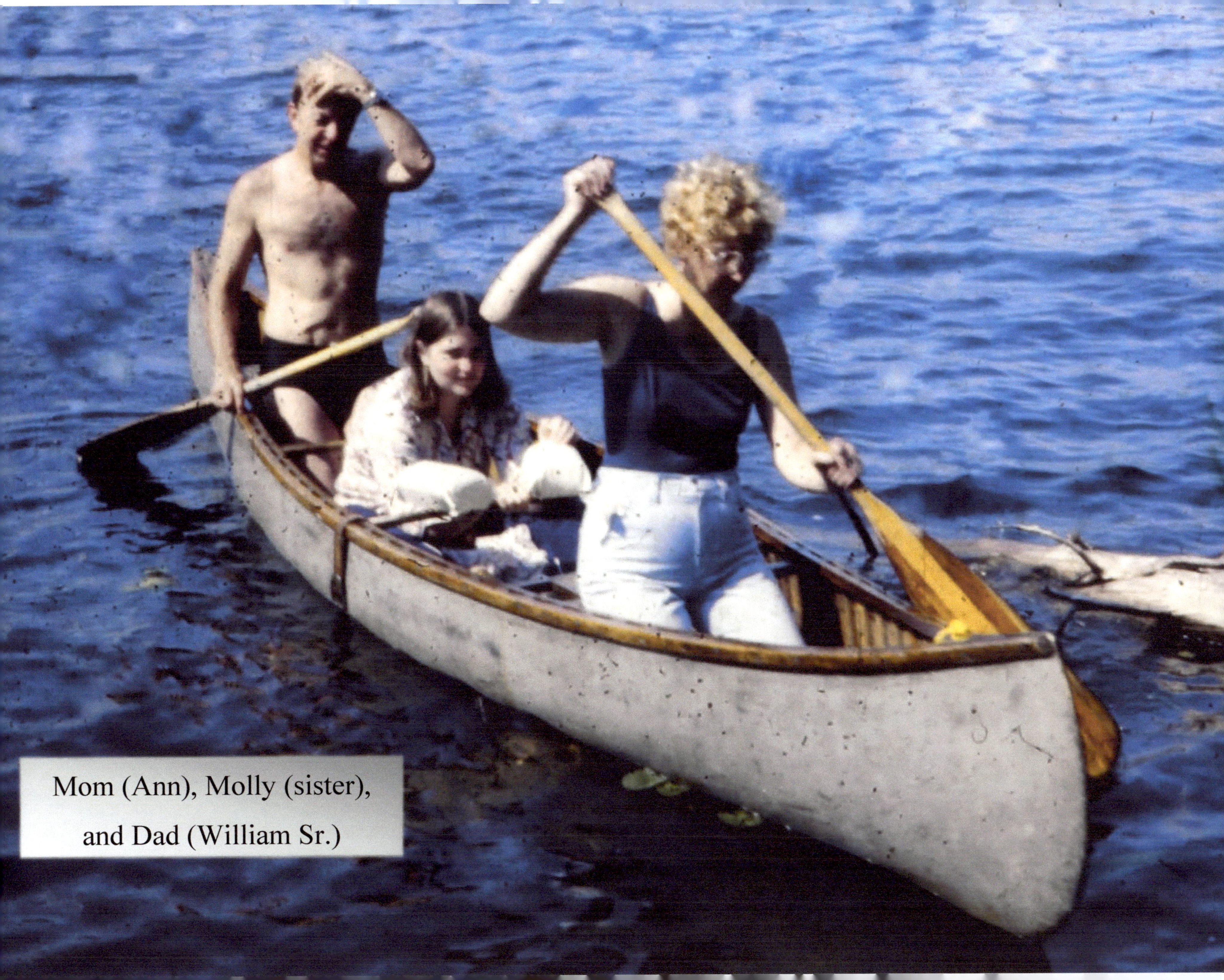

Mom (Ann), Molly (sister),
and Dad (William Sr.)

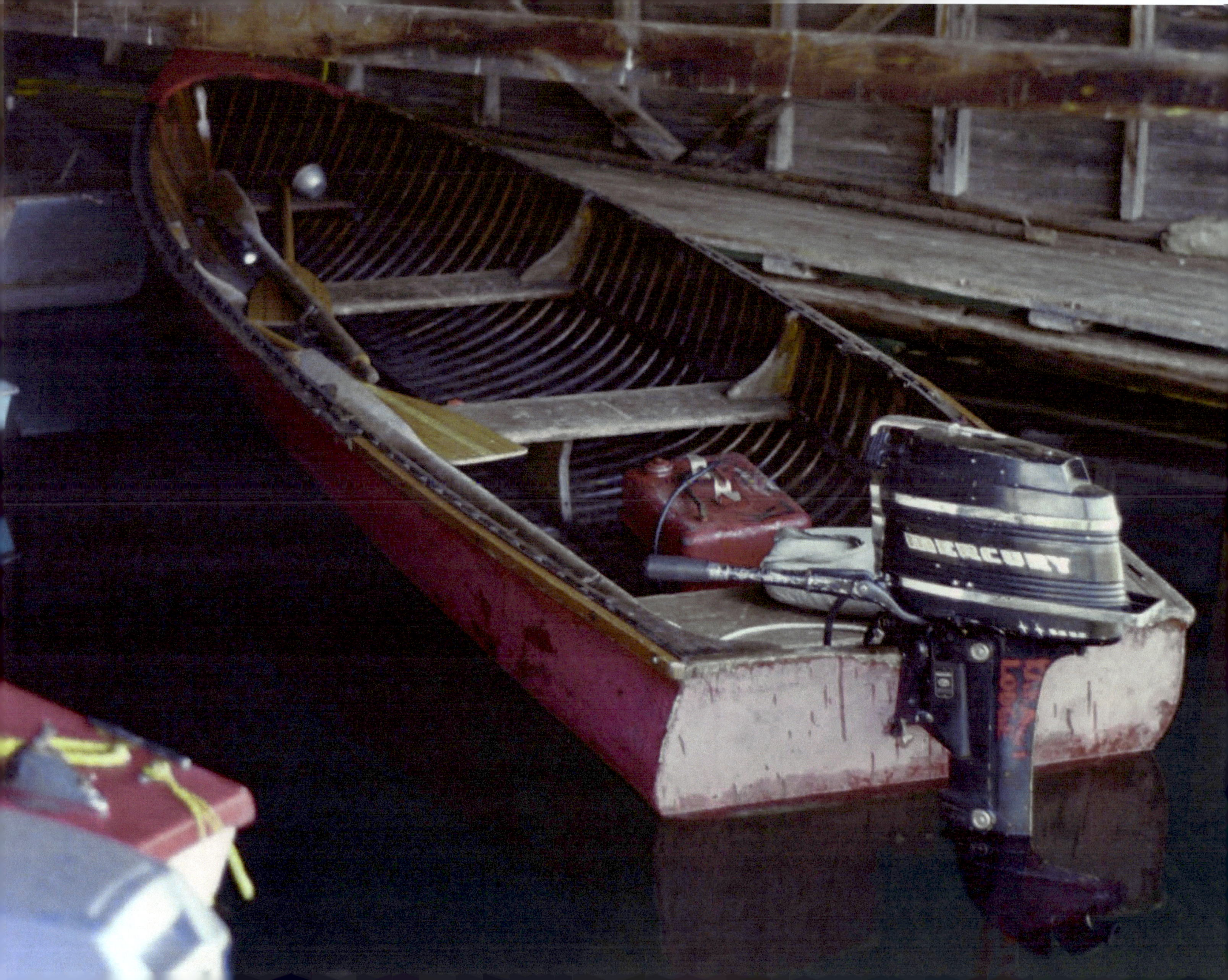
MERCURY

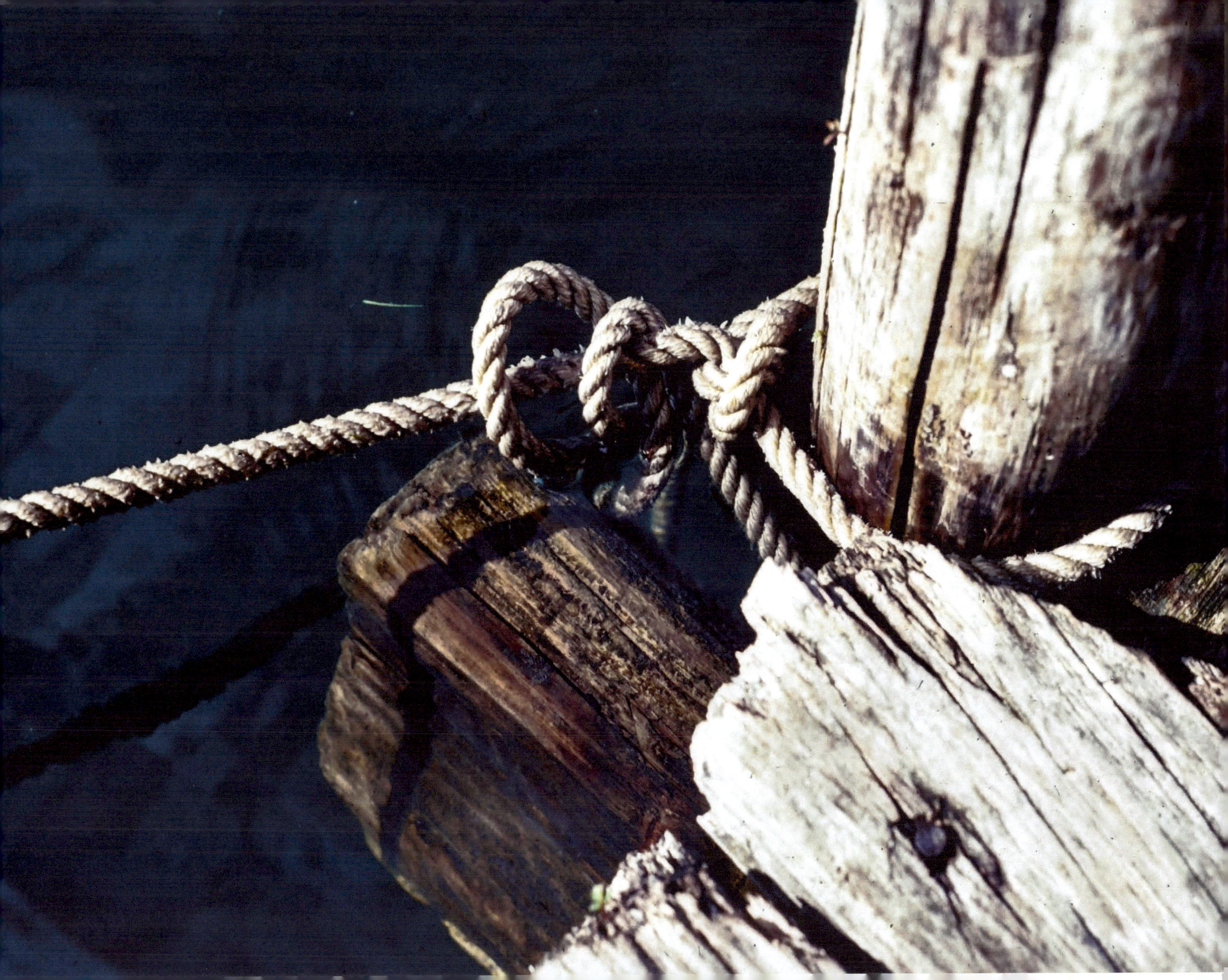

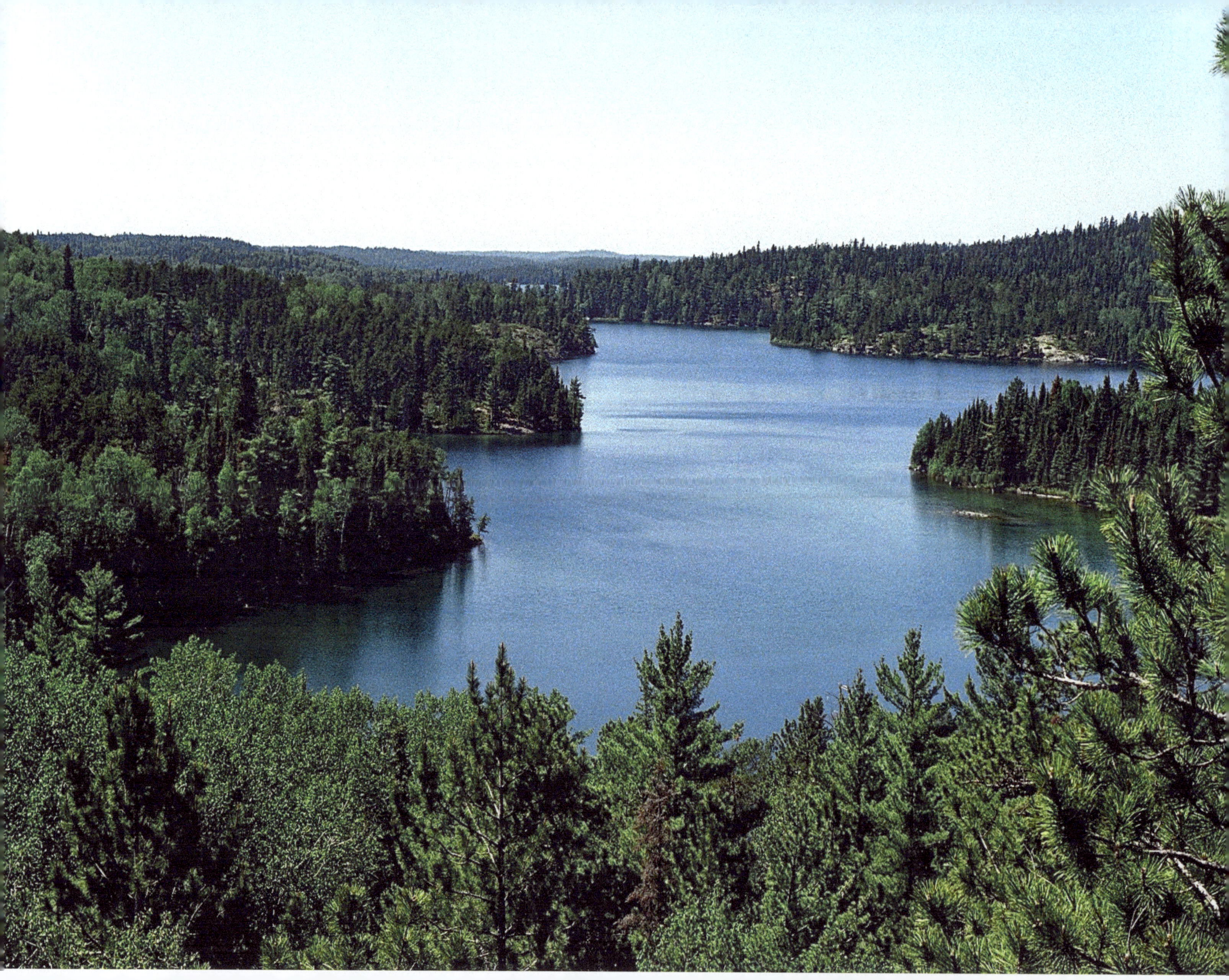

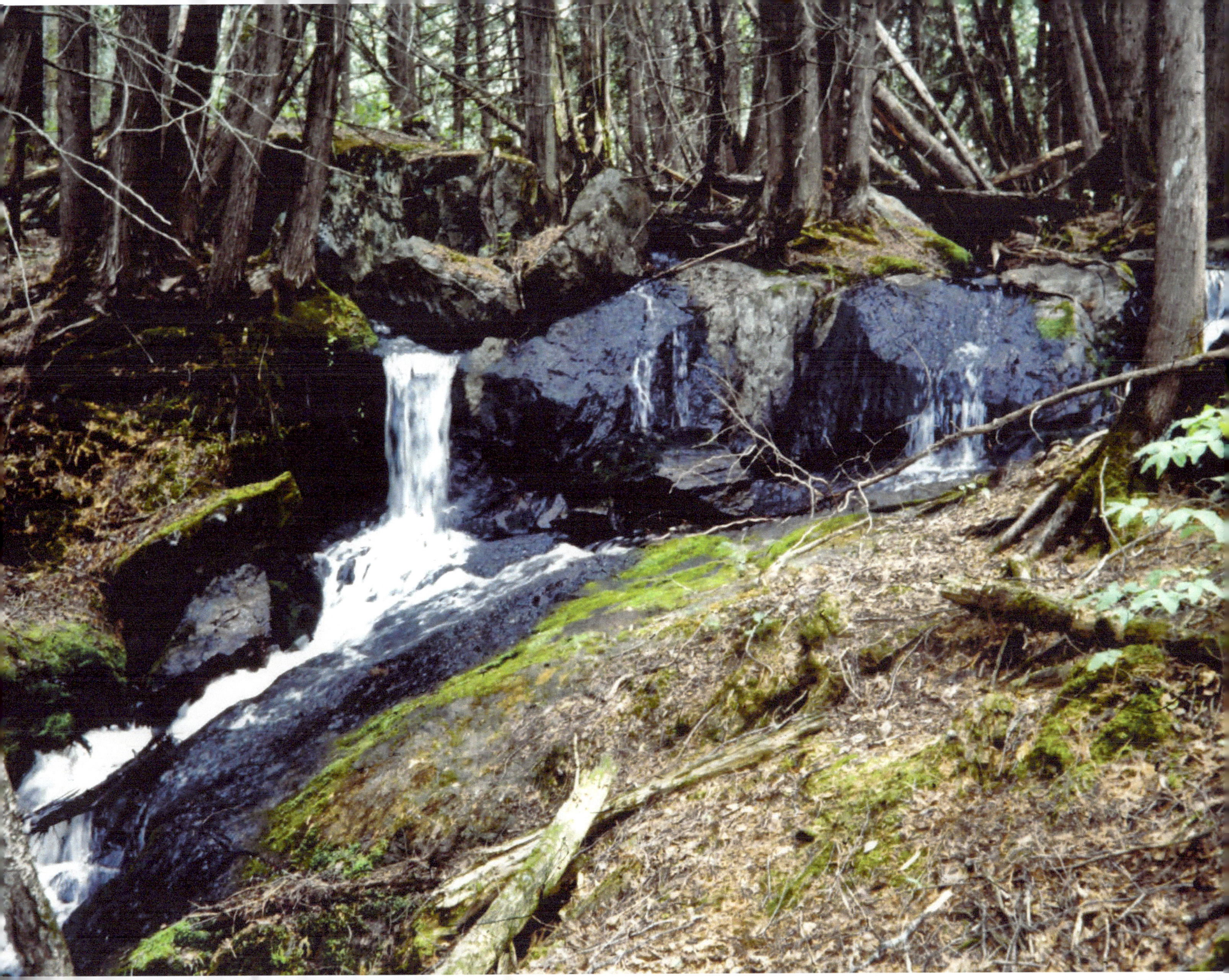

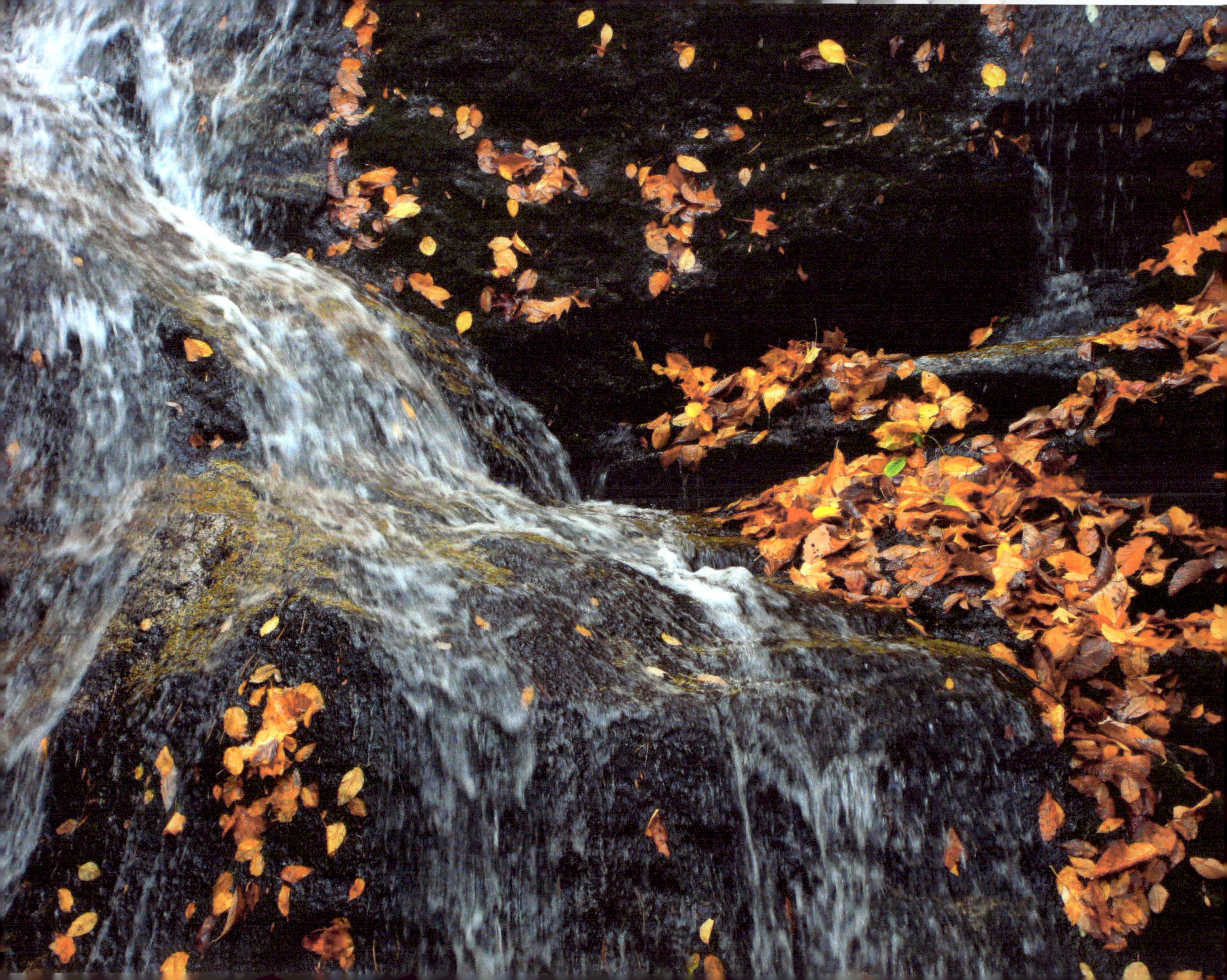

KAKAGI HOT FUDGE SAUCE

½ Cup Butter

4 Squares Baking Chocolate

3 Cups Sugar

1 Can Evaporated Milk

1 Teaspoon Vanilla

½ Teaspoon Salt

Melt butter and baking chocolate in saucepan over low heat. Once melted and mixed remove from heat.

Add the sugar to the melted ingredients.

Now slowly stir in the evaporated milk and heat slowly to just about boiling.

Stir continuously to keep it from burning.

While heating the sauce add salt and vanilla.

Once heated remove from burner and enjoy over your favorite ice cream.

MEN

Men are men, it matters not their race.

It matters not their skin color. It matters not their faith.

But still our world is filled with hate.

Some day there will be peace on earth.

With that all hate will cease.

That day will be the end, men no longer will exist.

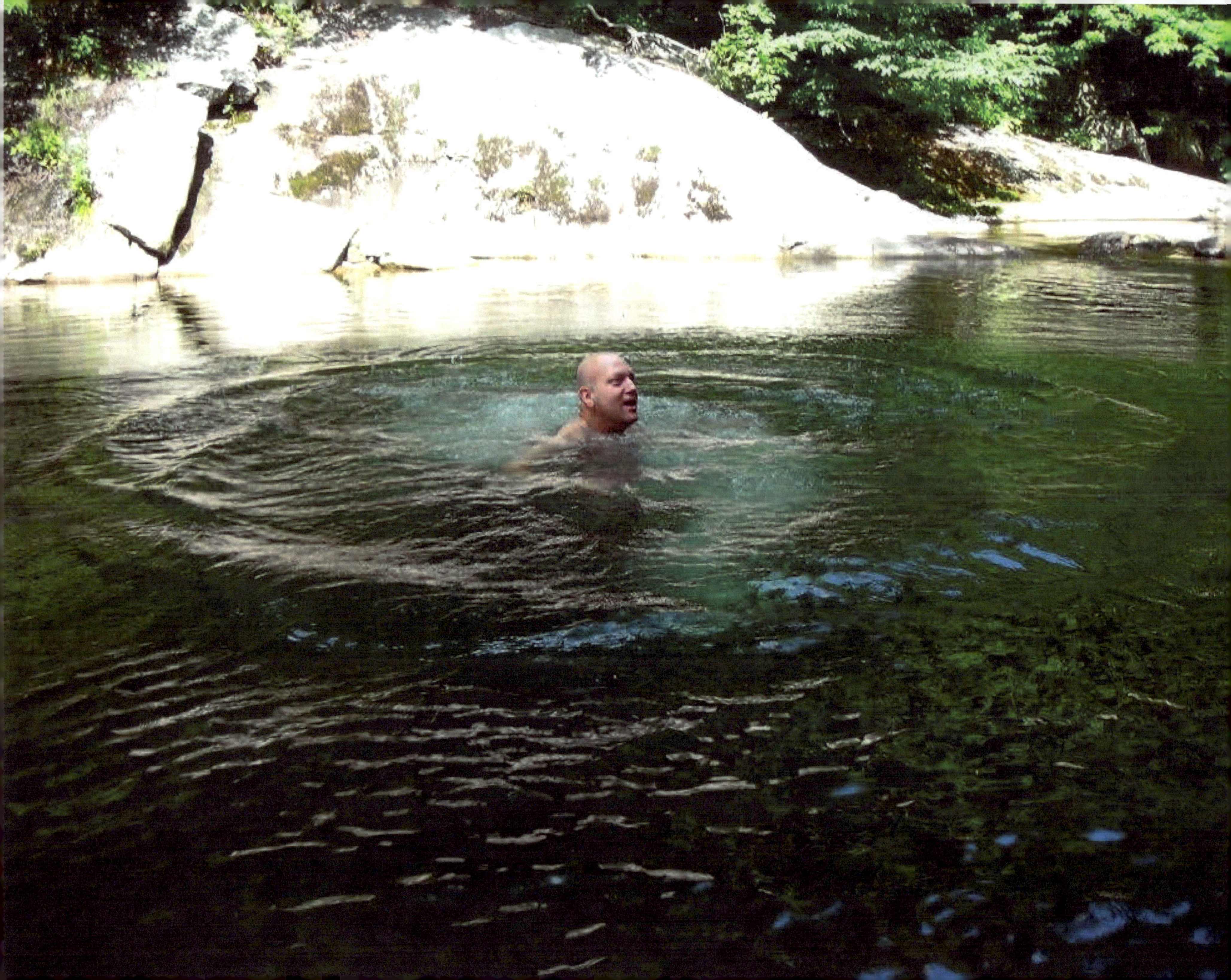

SILENCE

The woods they are so quiet with fresh snow upon the ground.

Like it was wrapped in cotton, listen, not a sound.

Listen to the silence, listen do you hear?

Oh, it is so quiet, oh it is so dear.

The trees are so enchanting, their branches piled with snow.

They bow down to silence.

Listen to it, oh!

Through the woods a stream is flowing it winds and wanders near.

See its rapids rushing, cascading, falling over ancient rocks made round.

Oh, what such beauty, but listen,

Silence, Not a sound.

In the tree a bird is singing.

Its song you cannot hear.

It is drowned out by silence.

Listen, do you hear?

The snow it falls like feathers, through the still night air.

All around the sounds of silence

Silence not a sound.

Walk through the woods so softly.

Walk through the woods with care.

Do not disturb the peaceful night.

Do not disturb the air.

The woods they are so quiet with fresh snow upon the ground.

Like it was wrapped in cotton listen, not a sound.

Listen to the silence, listen, can you hear?

Oh! It is so sacred.

Oh! It is so dear.

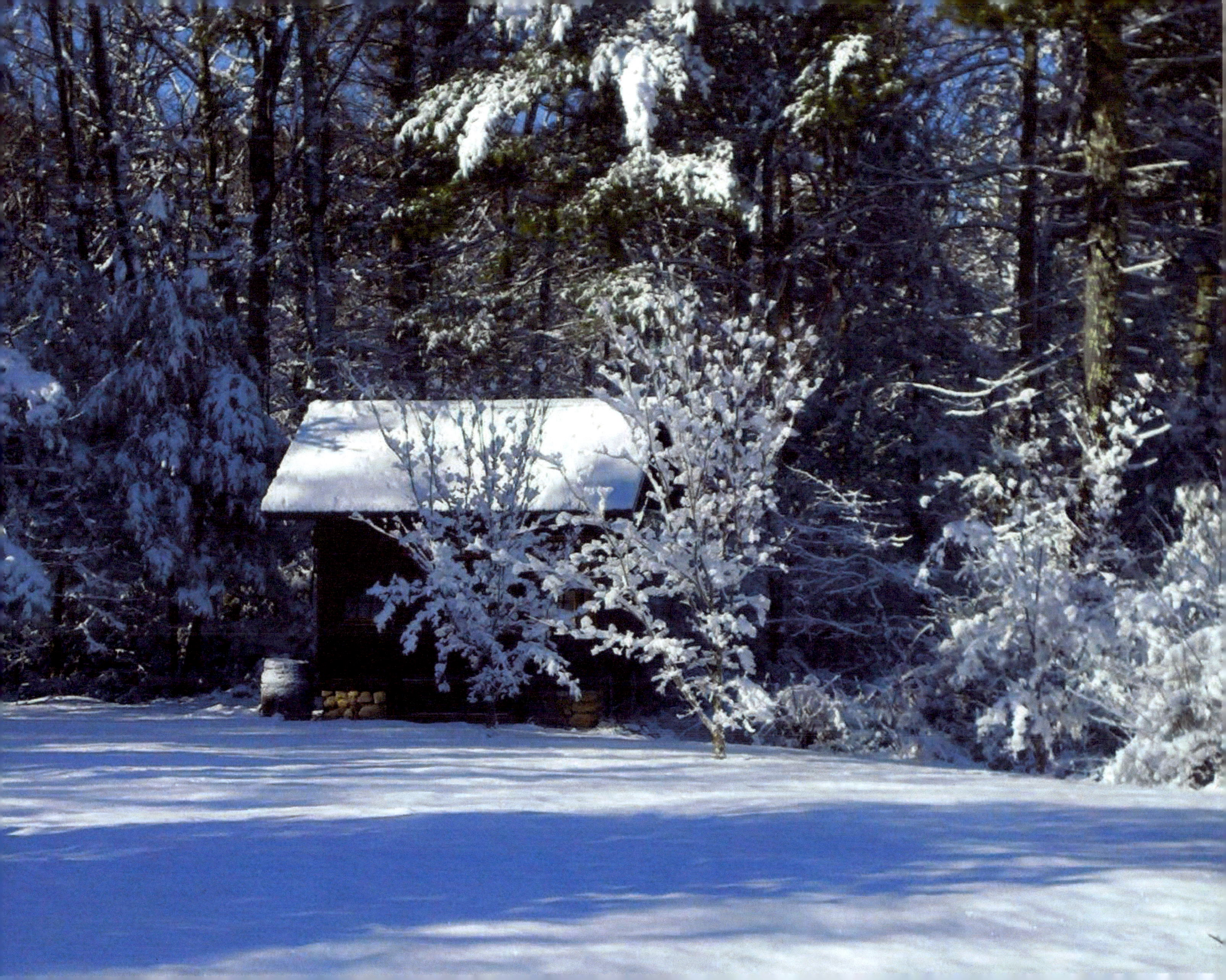

DAYDREAM

It was a cold windy day. The sun was rising in the east, casting light on the frozen landscape outside. I arose from my warm bed to the pink rays diffusing through my window. I heard the wind whistling through a crack in the floor and then scraped some frost off the window to have a look at the world outside. It had snowed during the night, and I could see drifts forming in the wind. The wind was alive. It seemed to have hands and to be shaping the snow into sculpture. I was now wide awake and began to move more rapidly in the cold air of my cabin. I left the wind and the frost covered window and began to go about my daily routine.

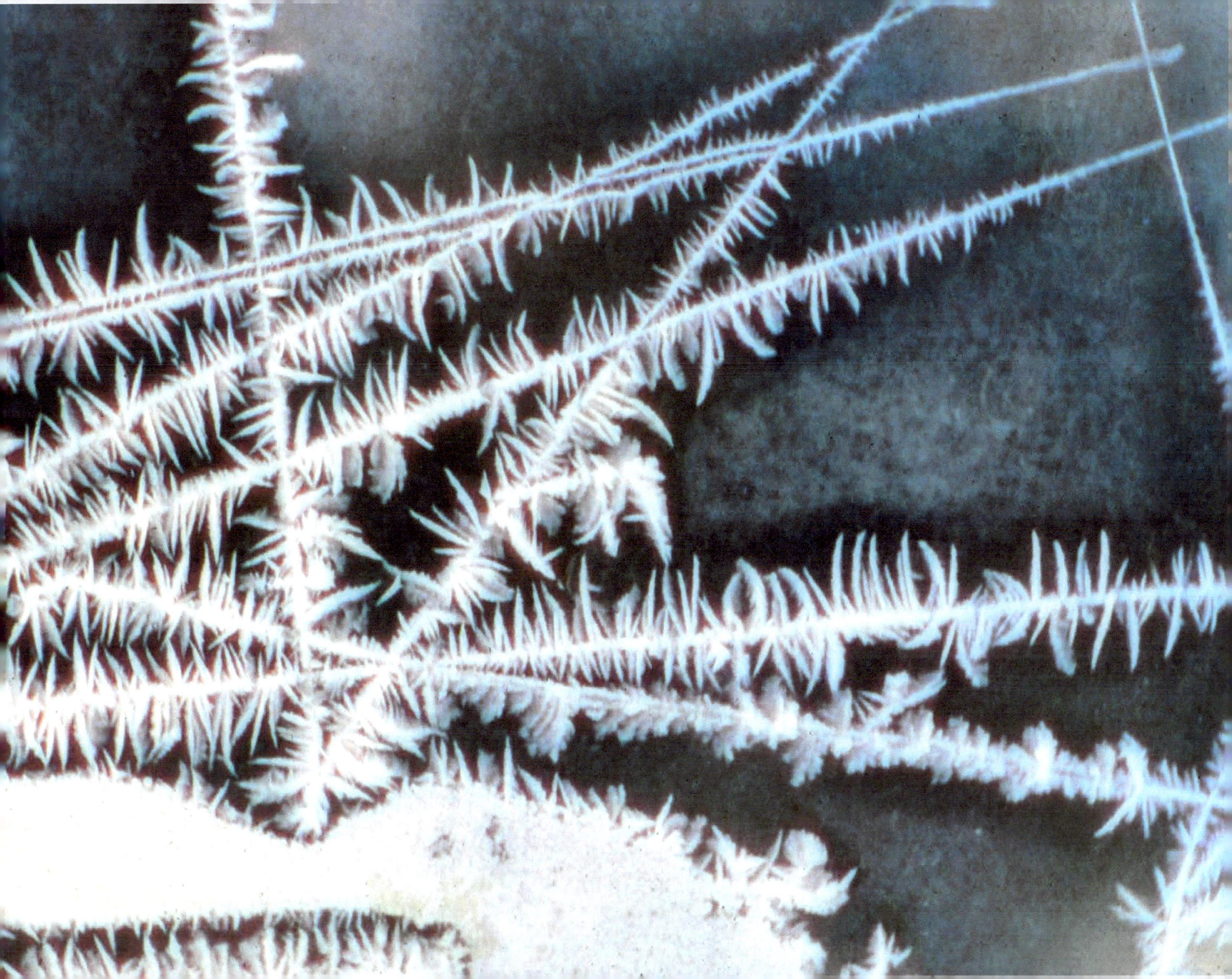

PARADISE NORTH

When the cool arctic air blows south on the breath of old man winter and the geese, high in the moon lit night, sing their songs, something stirs in me pulling me north to the land of laughing loons, rocky lakes, and towering pines. When the wind picks up, rustling the leaves, it too takes me back, back to that paradise north, where the summer days are long. The smell of a fire takes me back to the lodge and its warm crackling fire. Yes, I am there now. I can smell the pines. I can hear the loons. I can see the smoke as it streams from the lodge. Being here puts my mind at ease. When I am down and all alone this is the place I go. I walk through the woods or canoe the shoreline searching for the treasures of the lake.

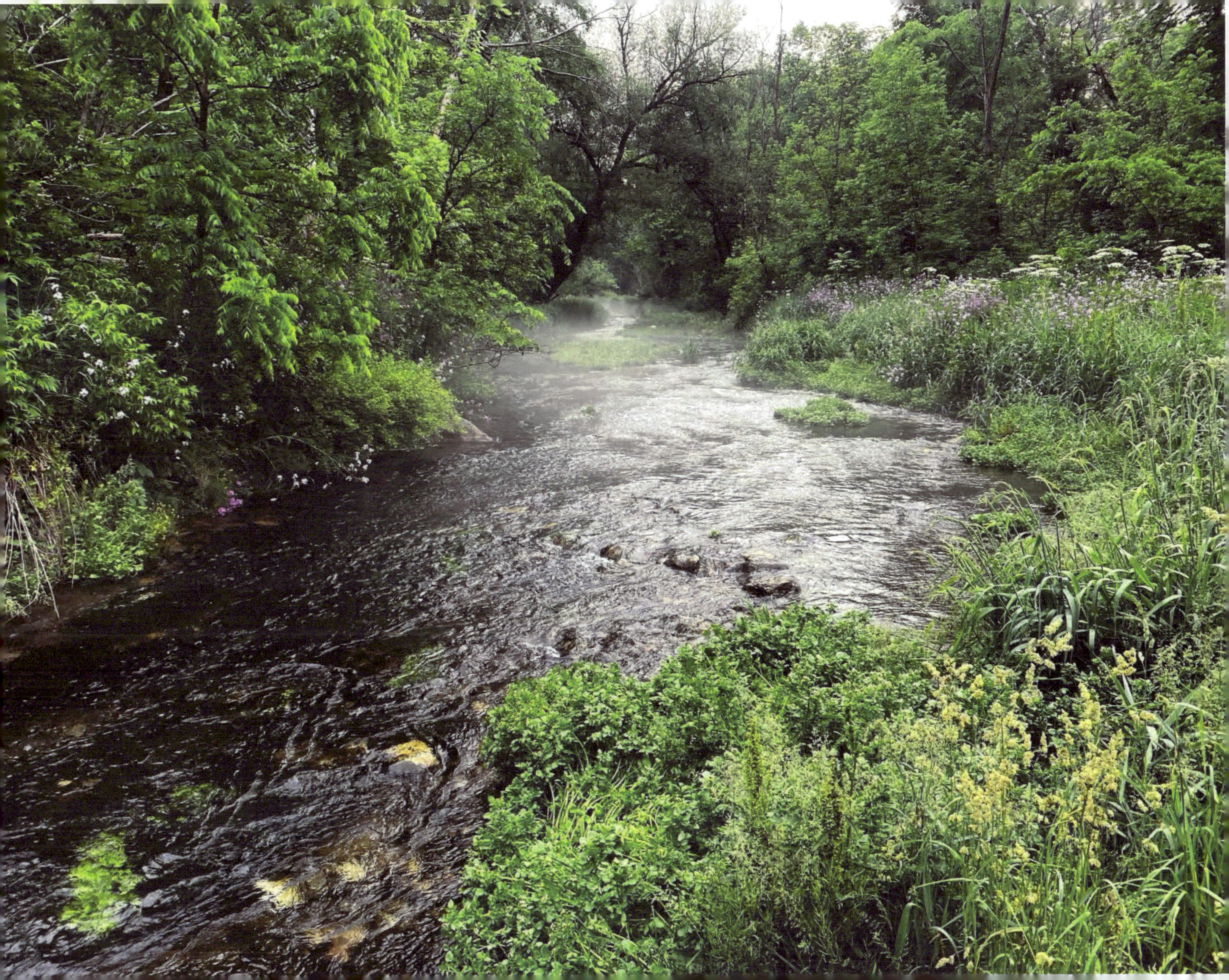

TIME

Time passes it ticks away.

I try to stop it, but it flies away.

I try to slow it but older I grow.

And when I am bored with nothing to do, the hands of the clock, they no longer move.

Time passes it ticks away.

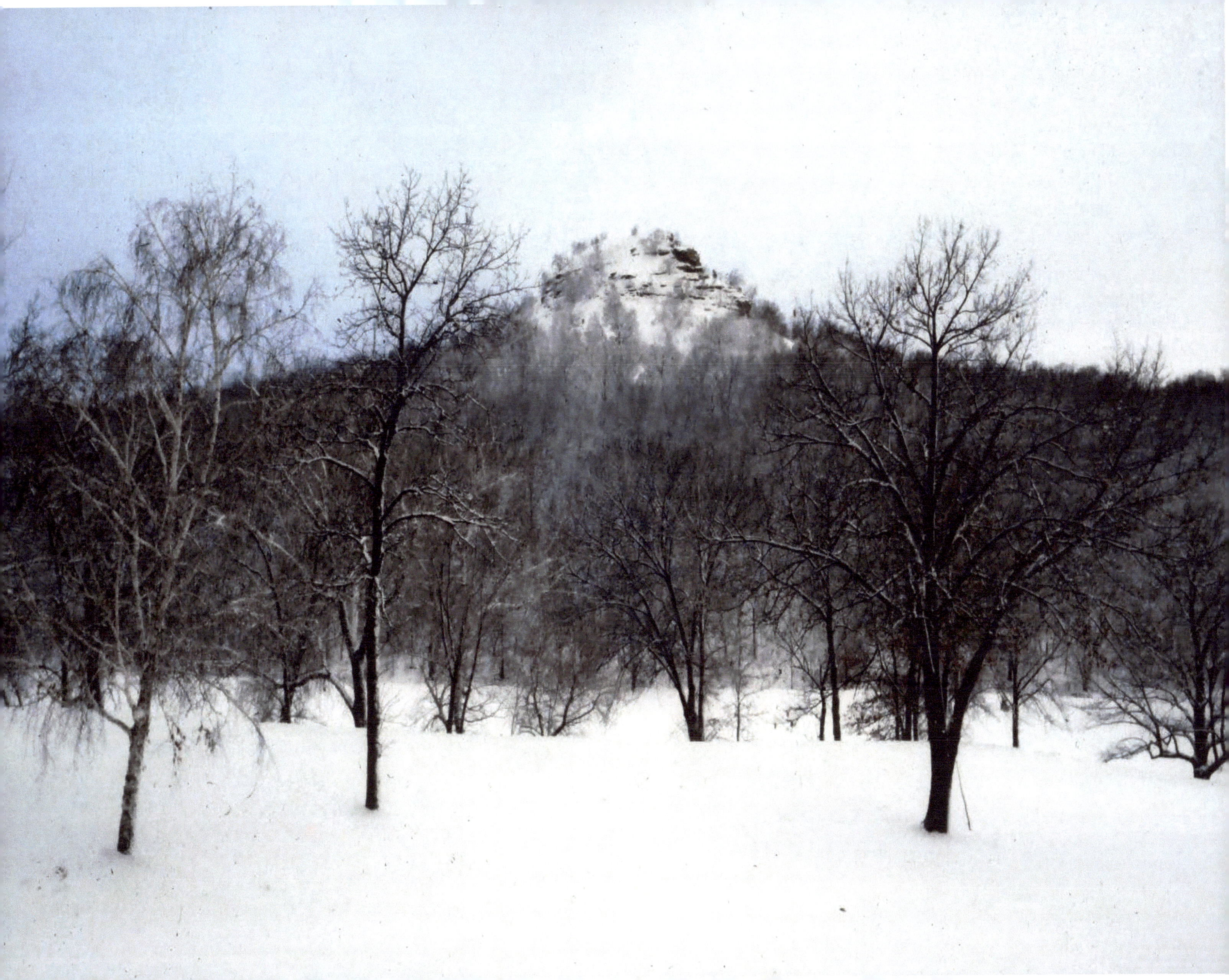

CRY AND PRAY

I've been lonely since you've gone. Nothing seems to ease the pain.

I cry and pray and think of you and wish our lives could be renewed.

But I know that will not take place, so I cry and pray in this lonely place.

The nights, they are the worst for me, the darkness holds no sympathy.

So, I cry and pray. I fall asleep, then wake again to a lonely day.

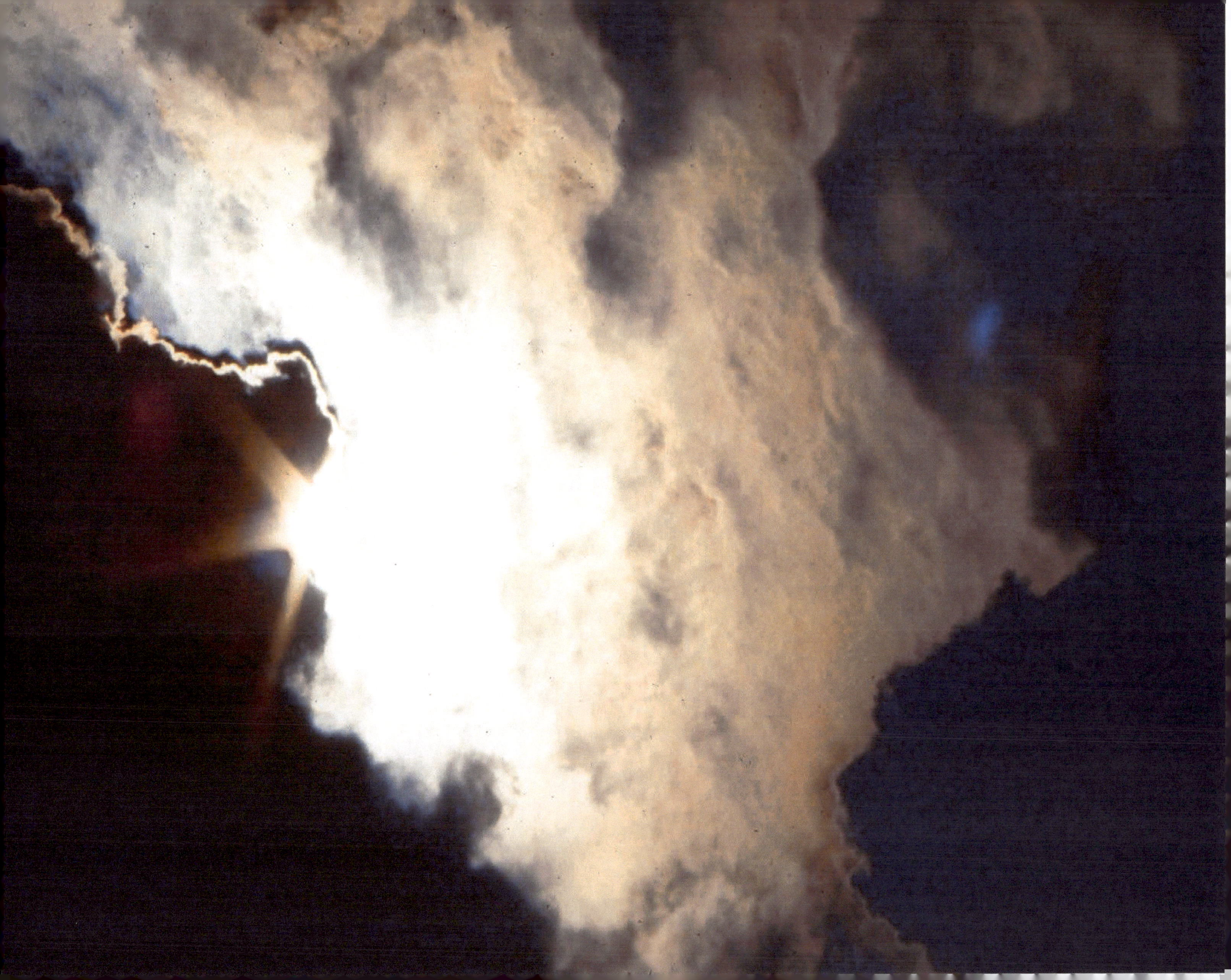

SOMEWHERE

Some where there is a valley with a river running wide and deep.

Its banks are lined with bluffs, with sides that are so steep.

Down in this valley, the trees are always green.

And the sweet smell of wildflowers makes the air smell, so fresh and clean.

The wind there it blows gently, there are no violent storms.

And there, my little Mitzy, roams free, for evermore.

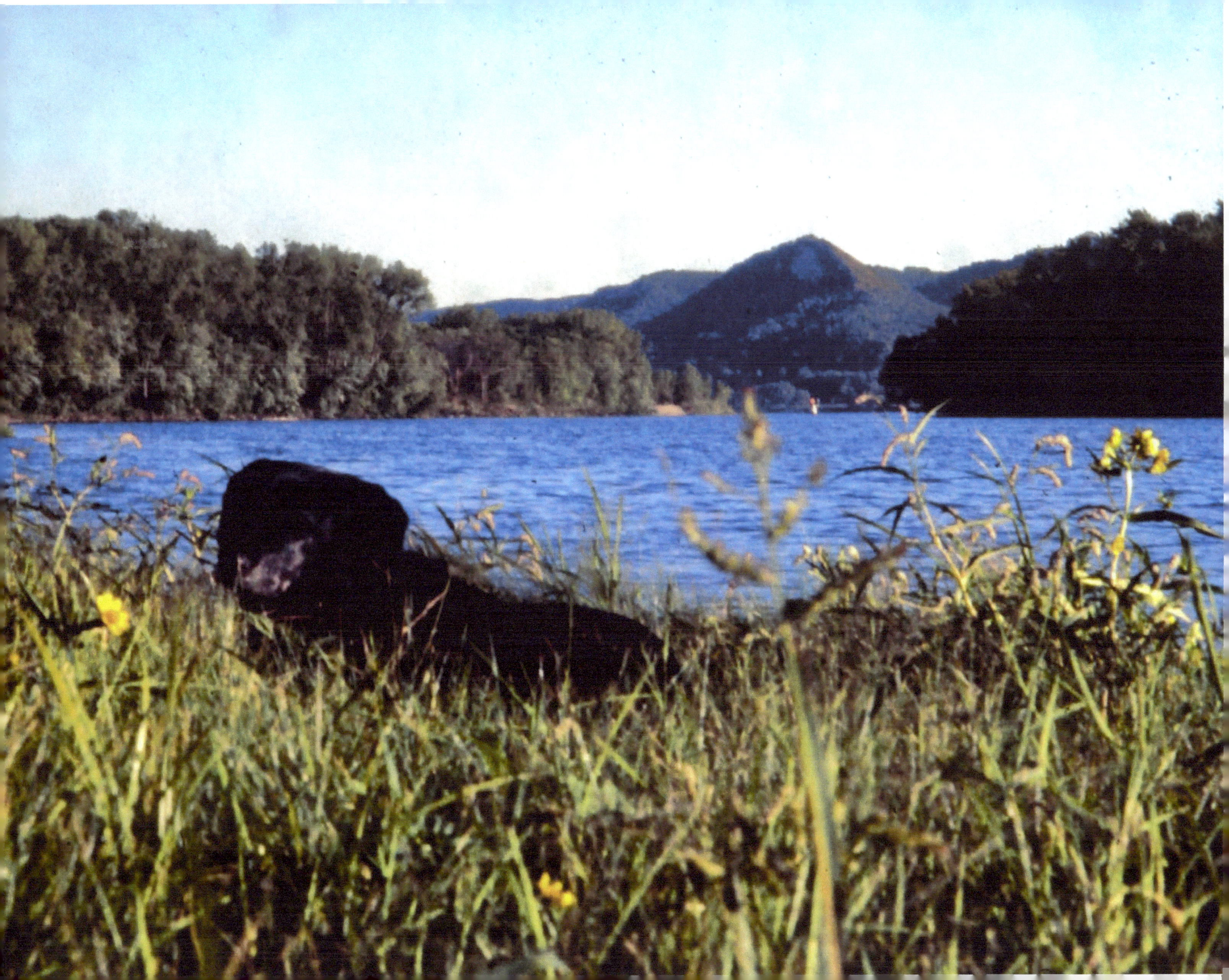

IF

If I were you and you were me, I wonder how this world would be?

Would you do the things I did to you? Would I do the things you did to me?

If I were you and you were me?

Would our kids play with guns out in the street, and call each other enemy?

If I were you and you were me?

If we'd trade places for just a day, perhaps we'd see things a different way?

If I were you and you were me?

But I'm not you and you're not me.

I hate you and you hate me, so I guess we'll never see how thing could be?

I guess it's sometimes nice to dream.

If you were me and I were you there's no telling what things we could do?

I guess it's up to me and you.

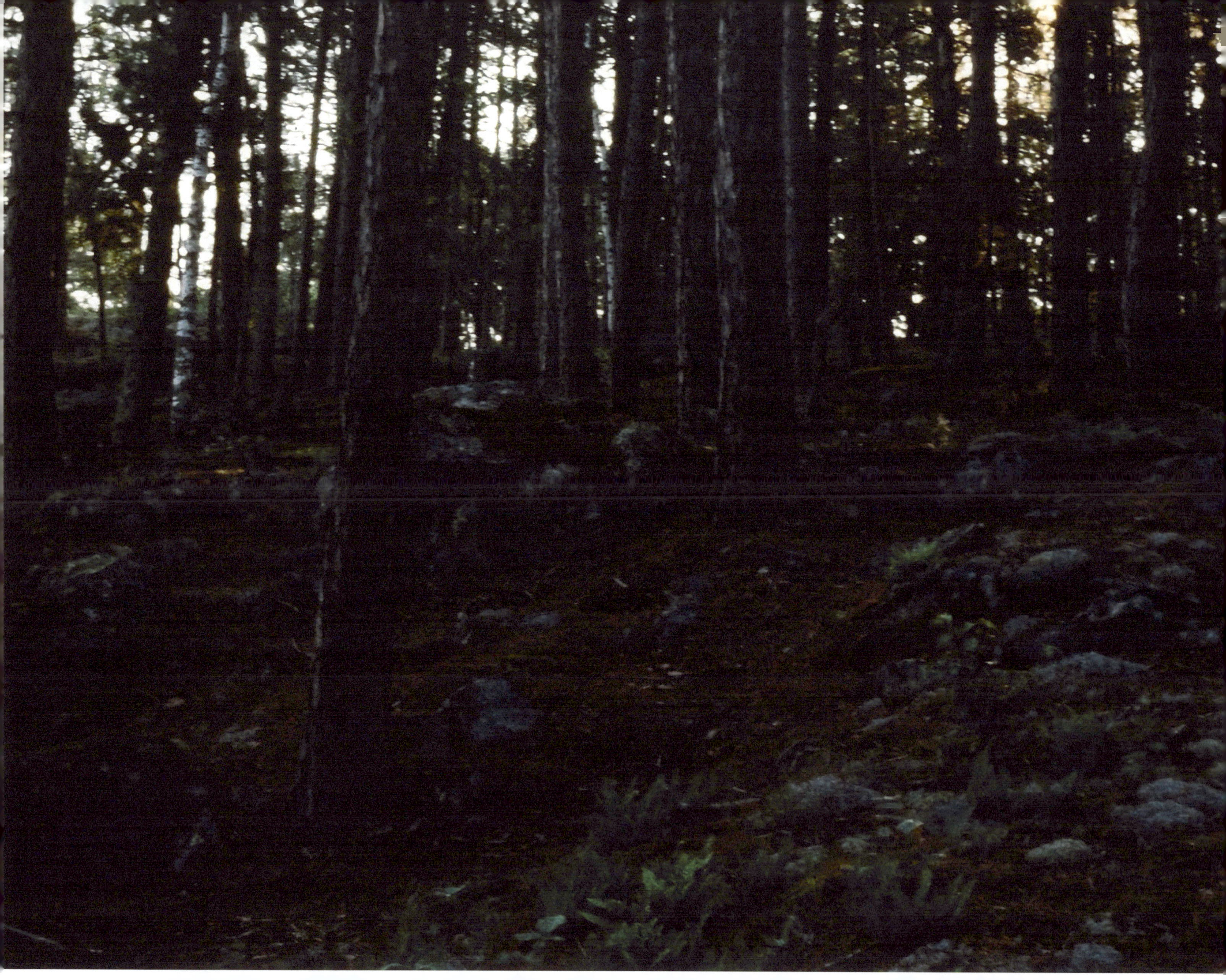

William D. Van Atta Jr.:

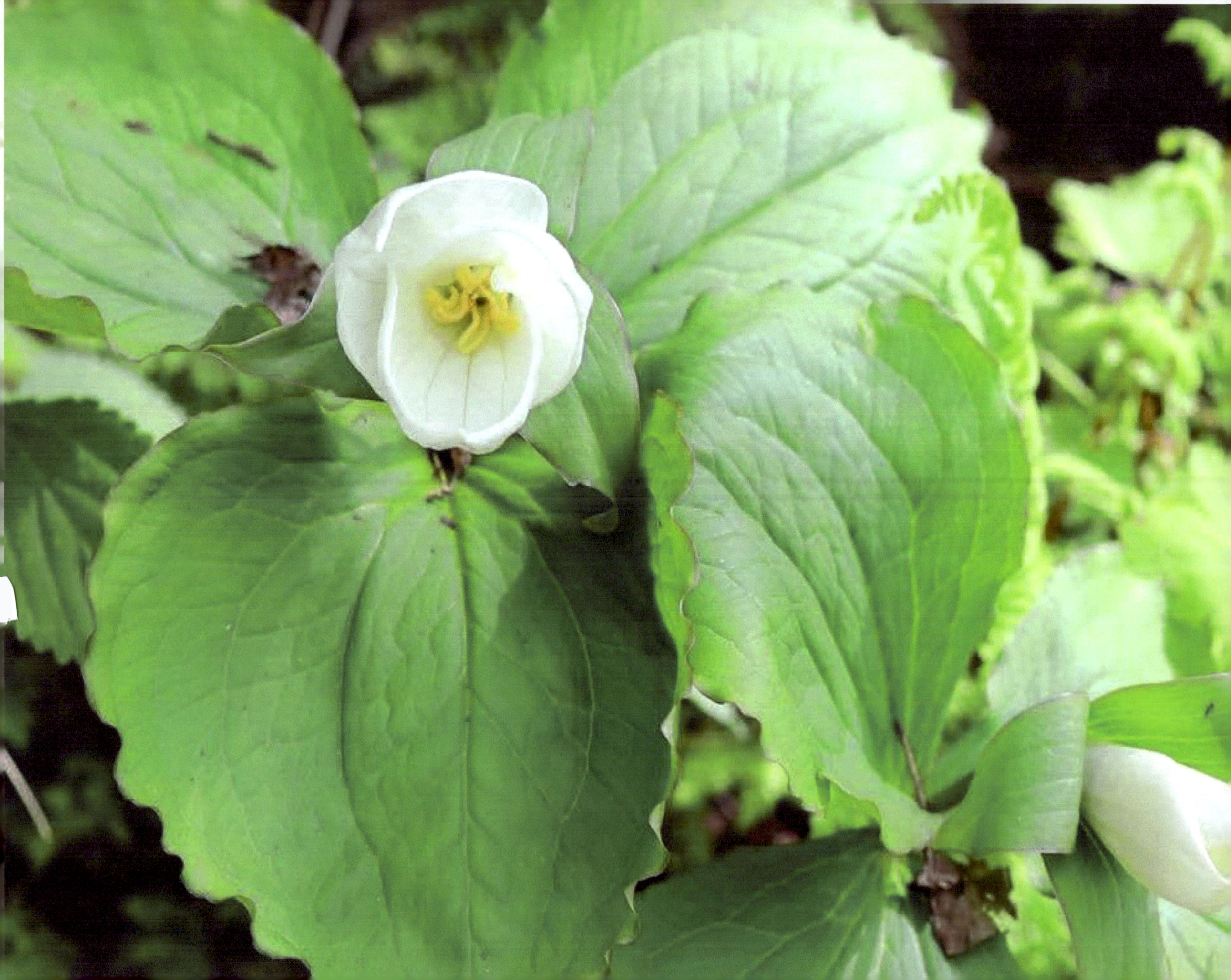

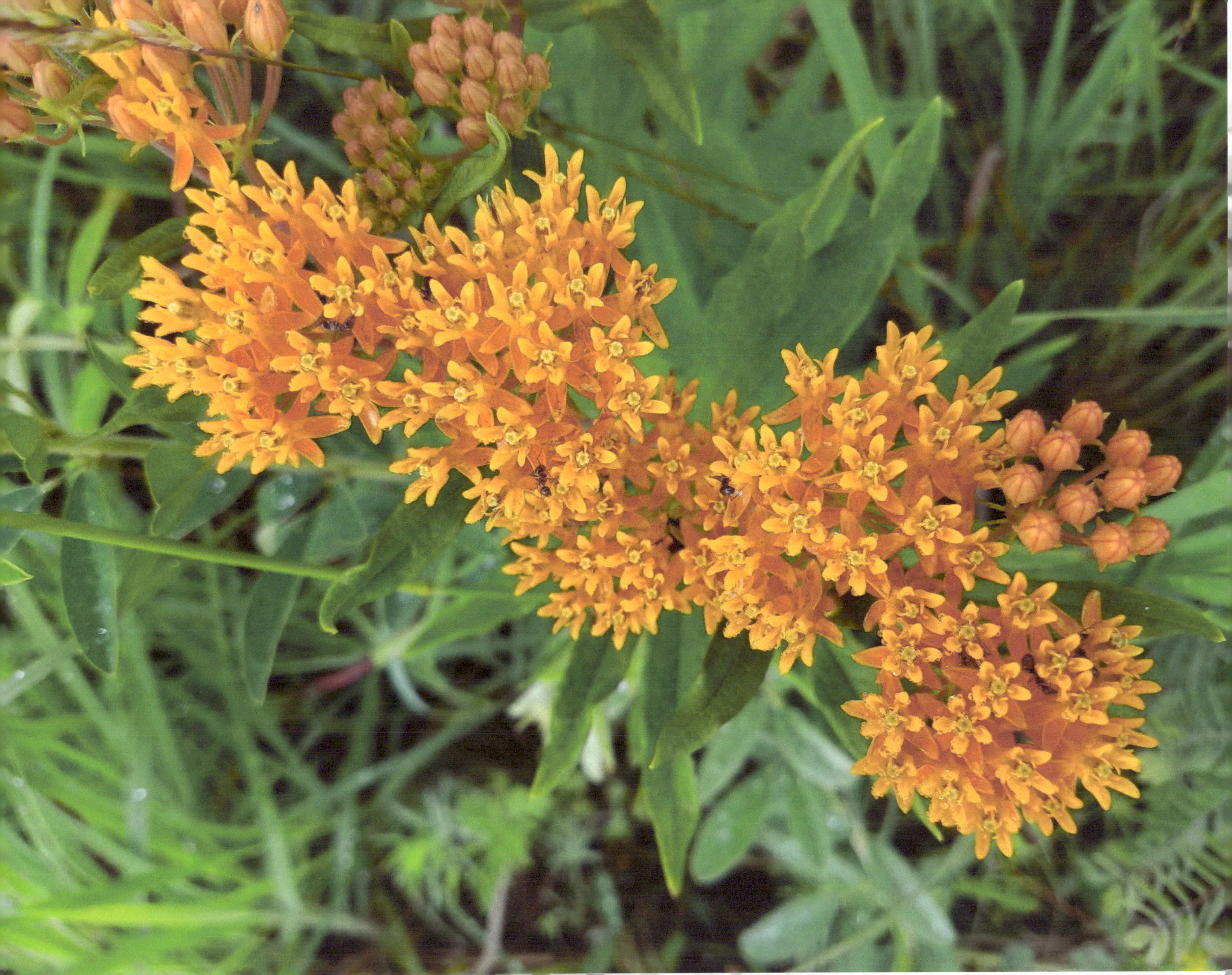

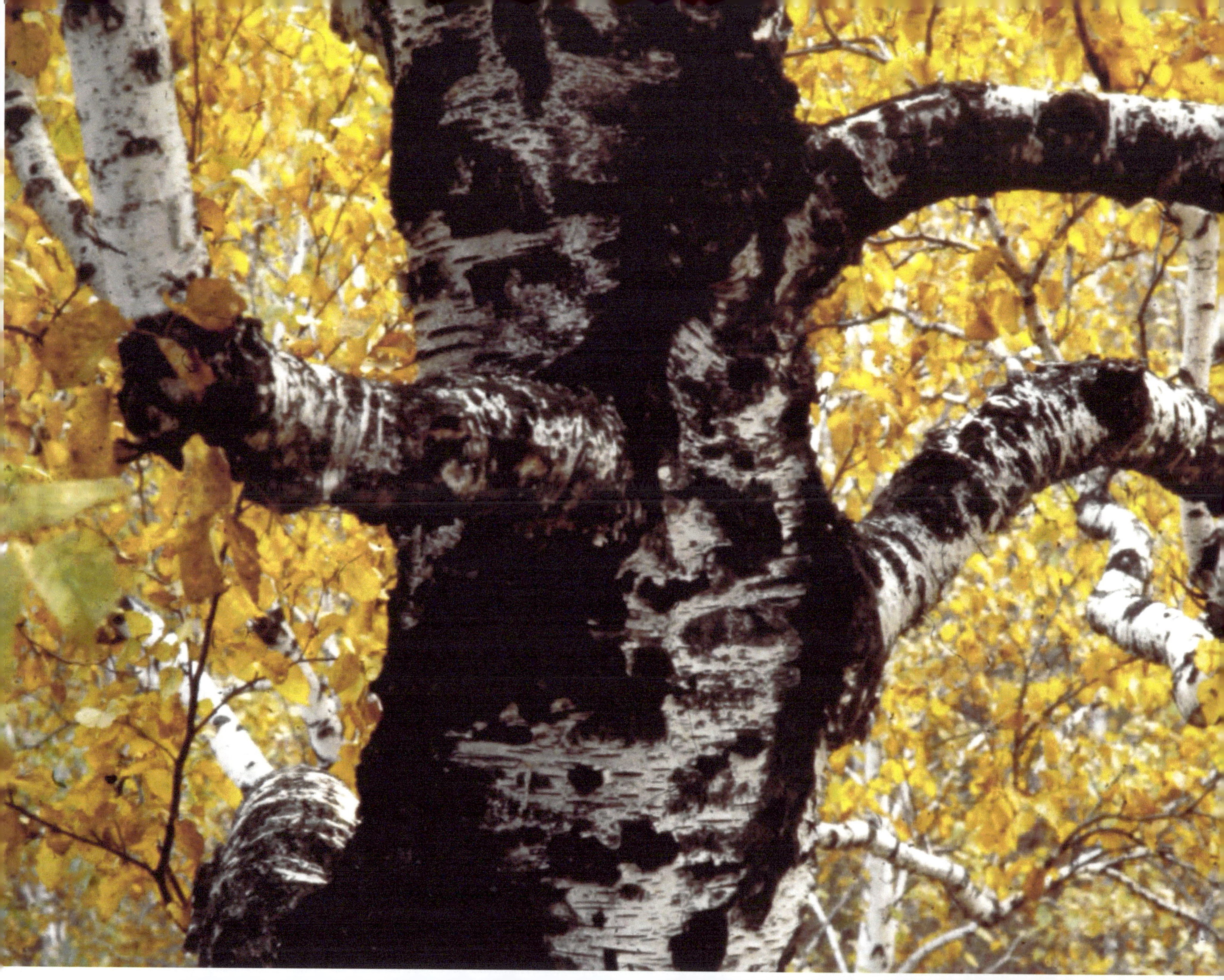

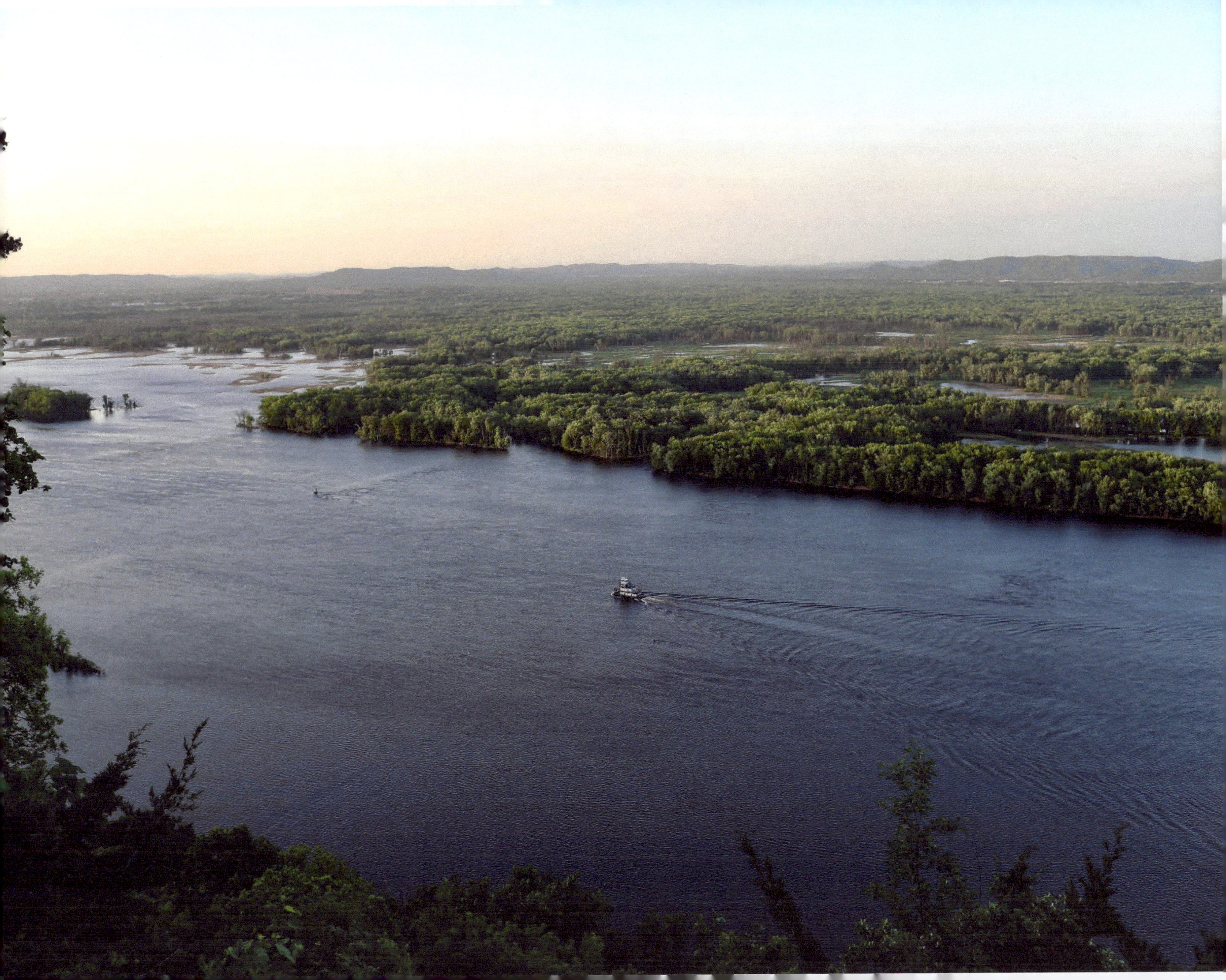

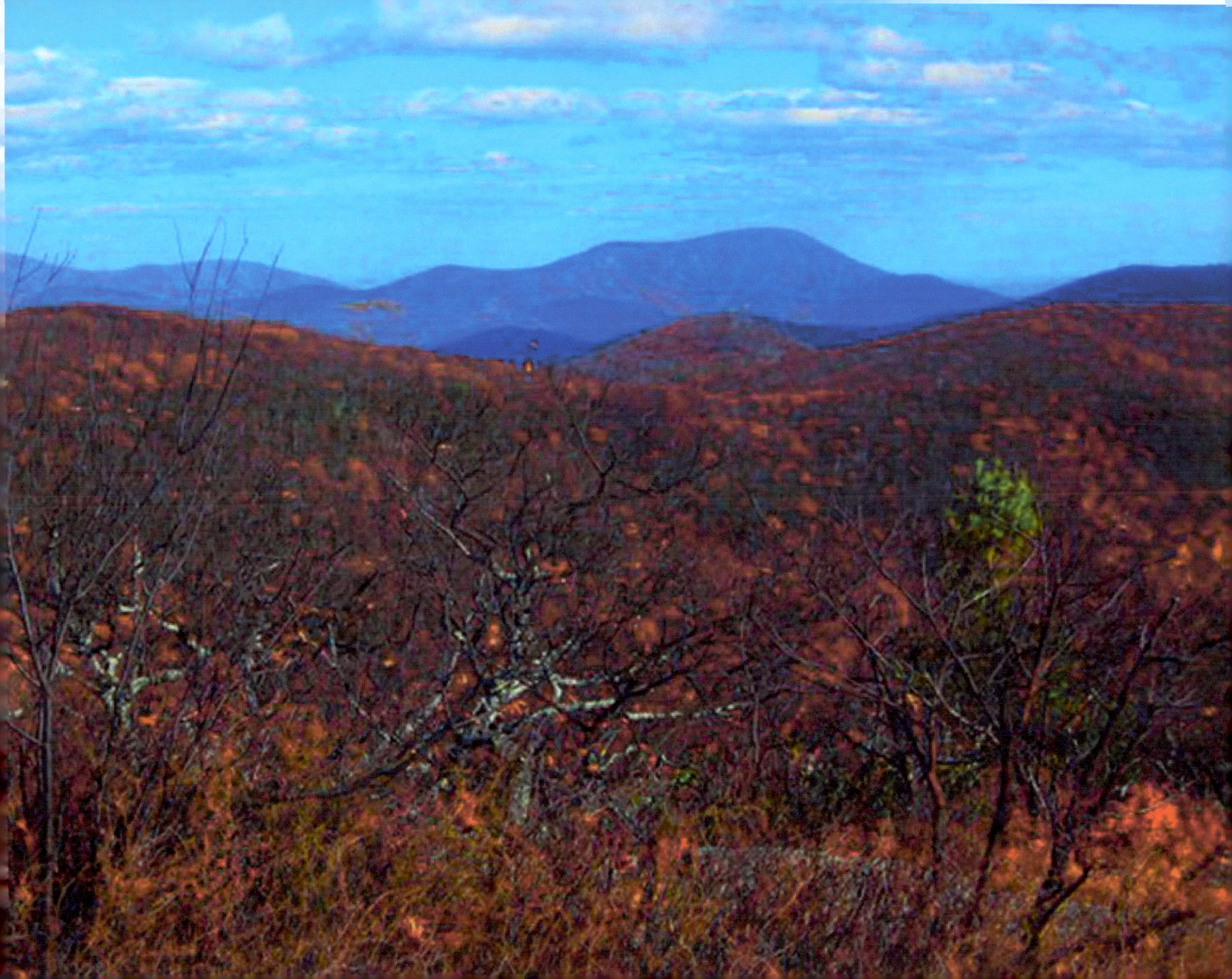

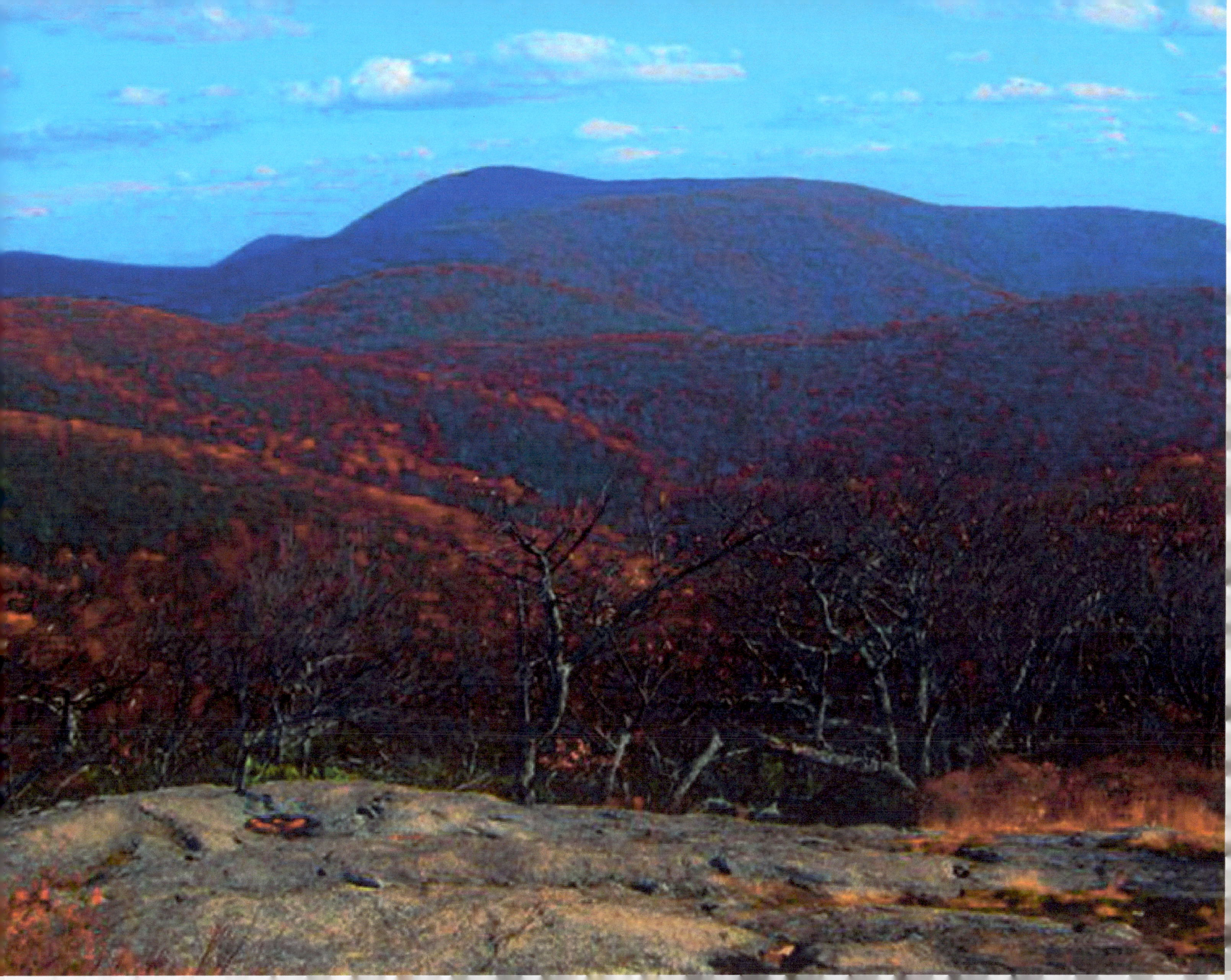

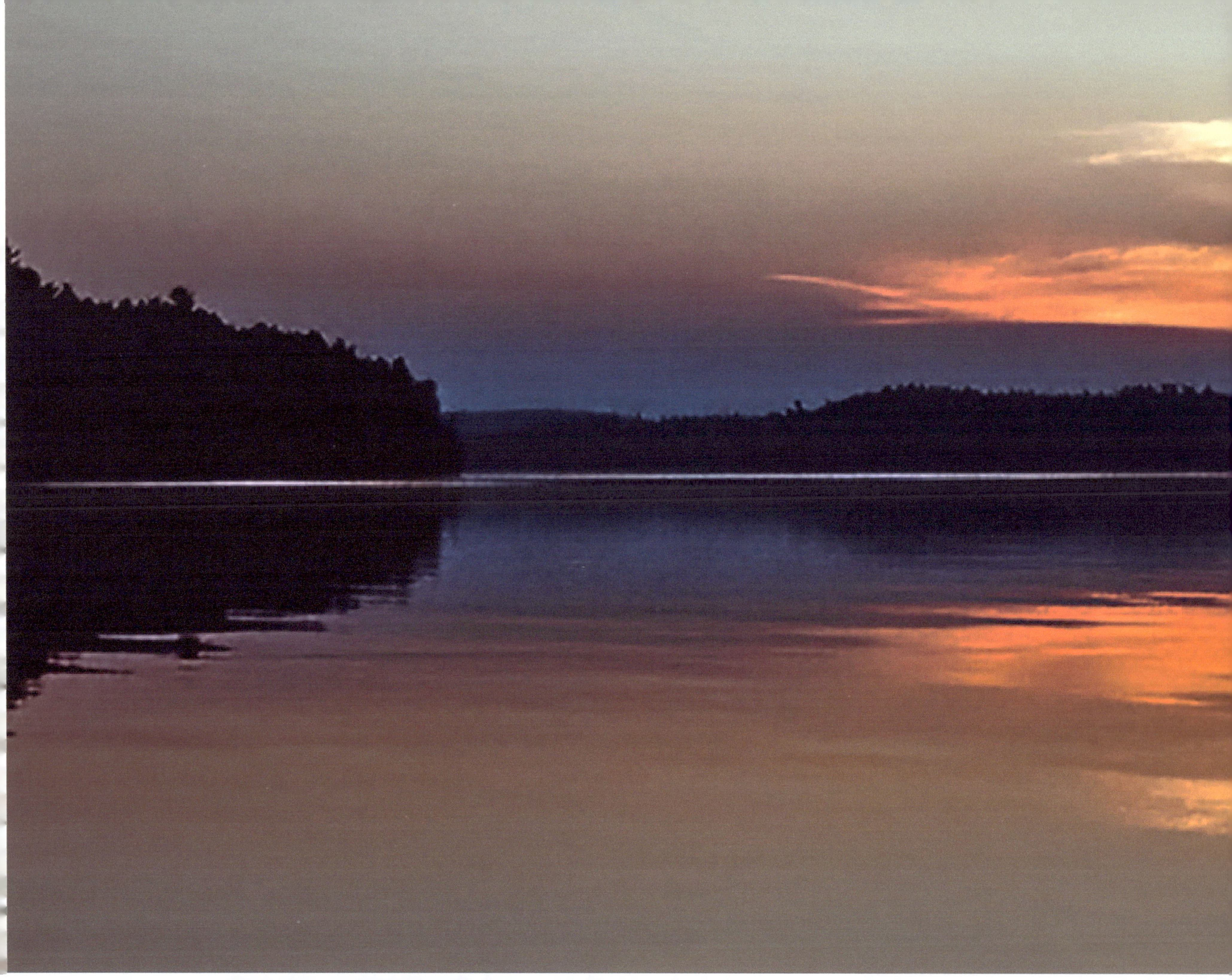

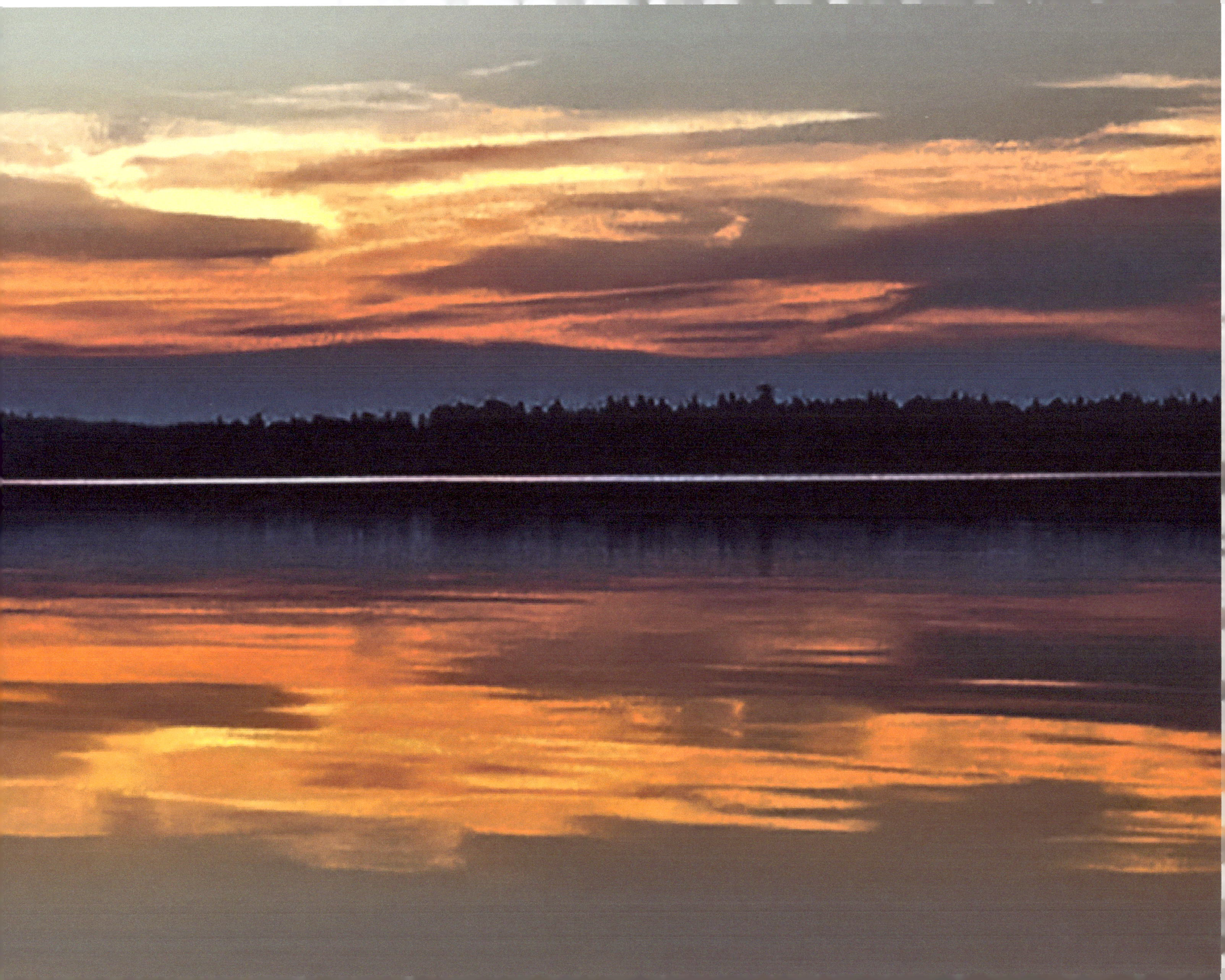

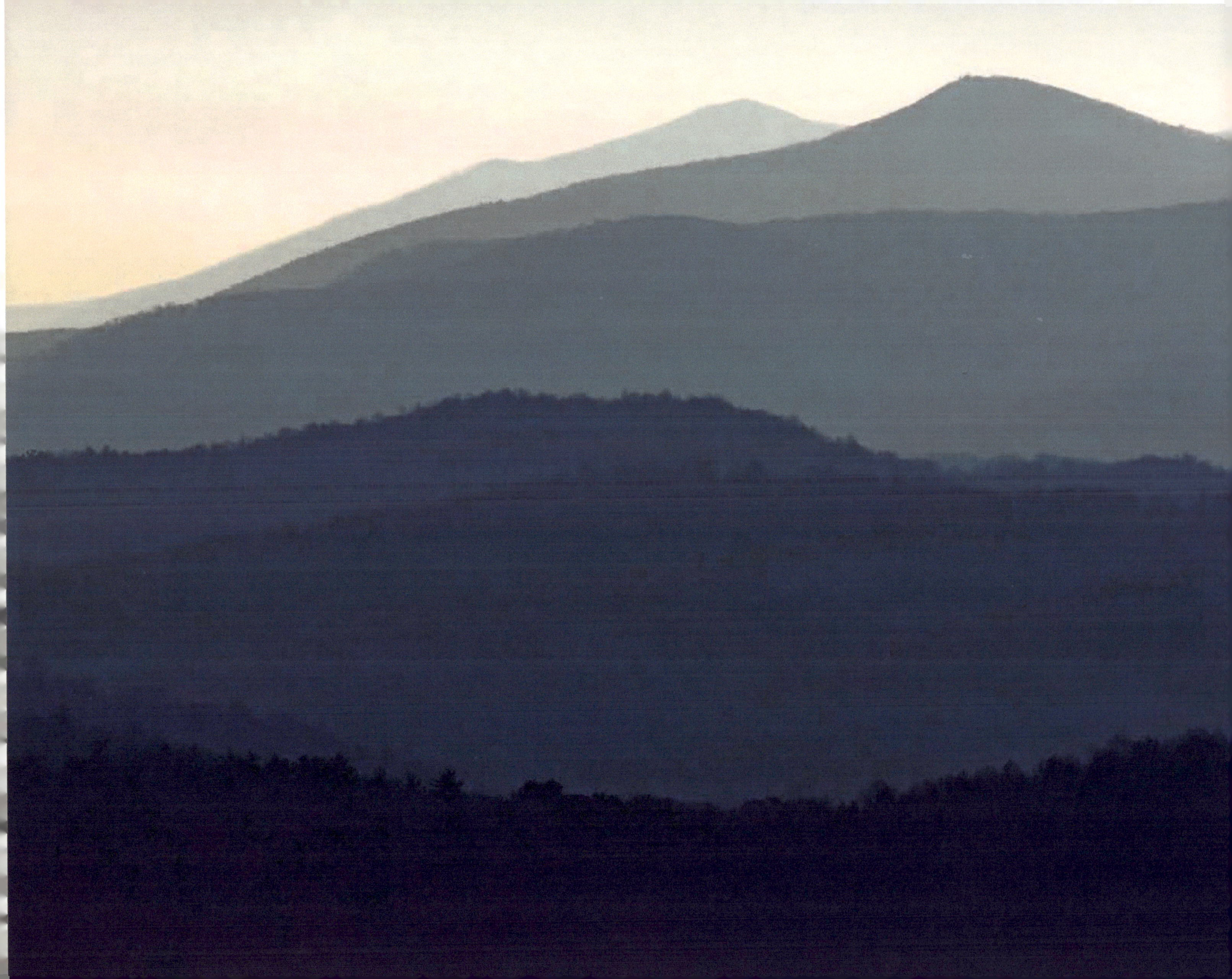

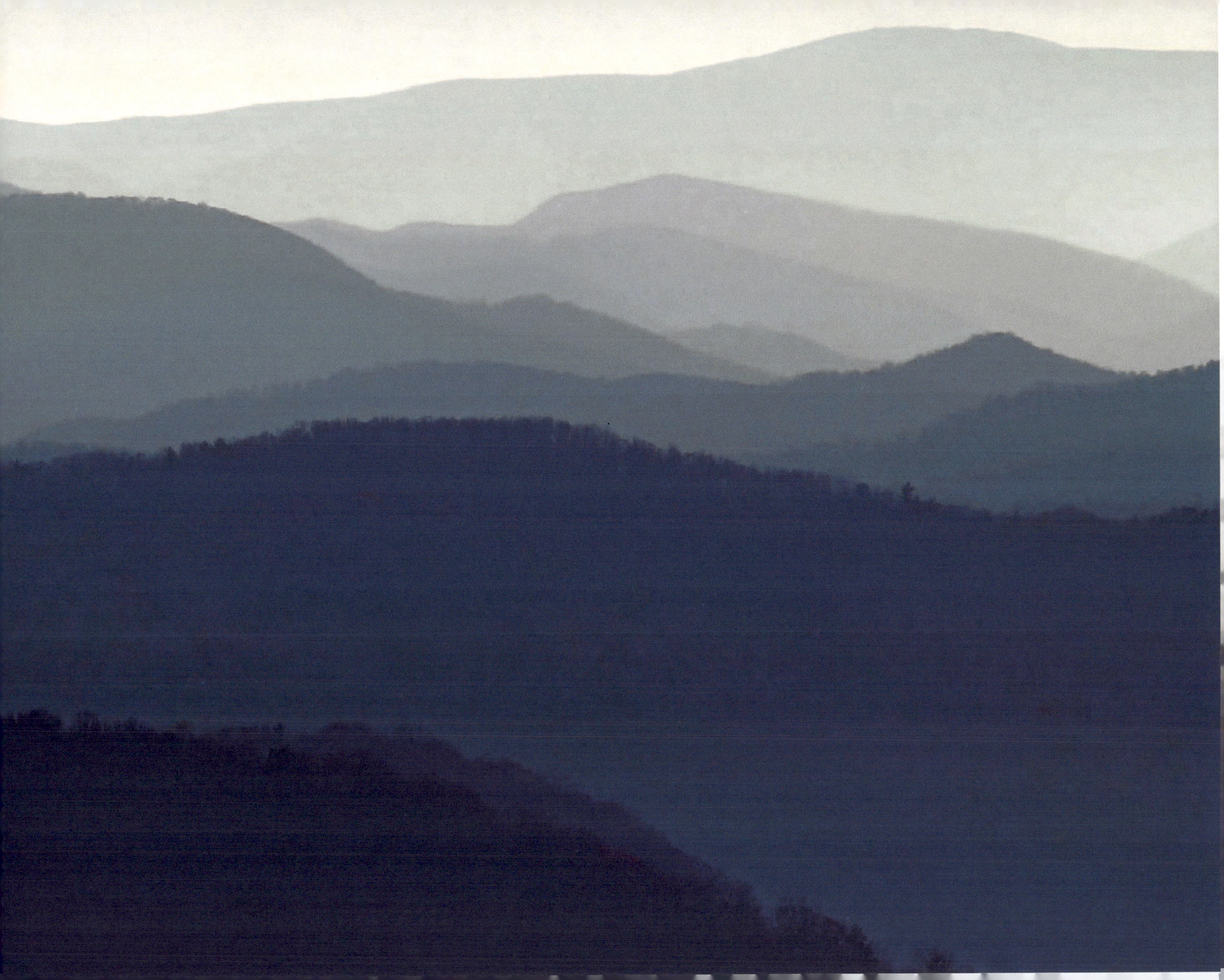

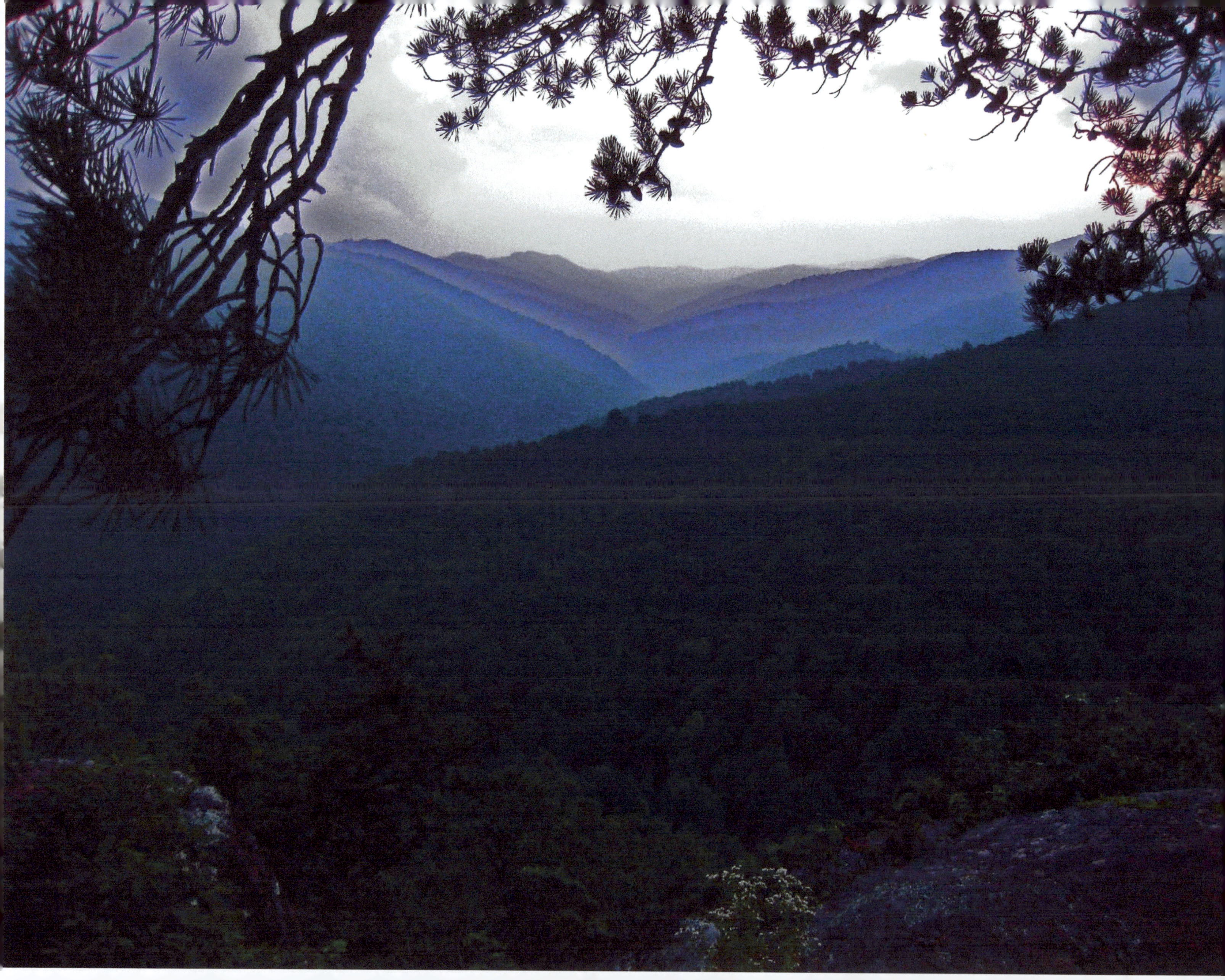

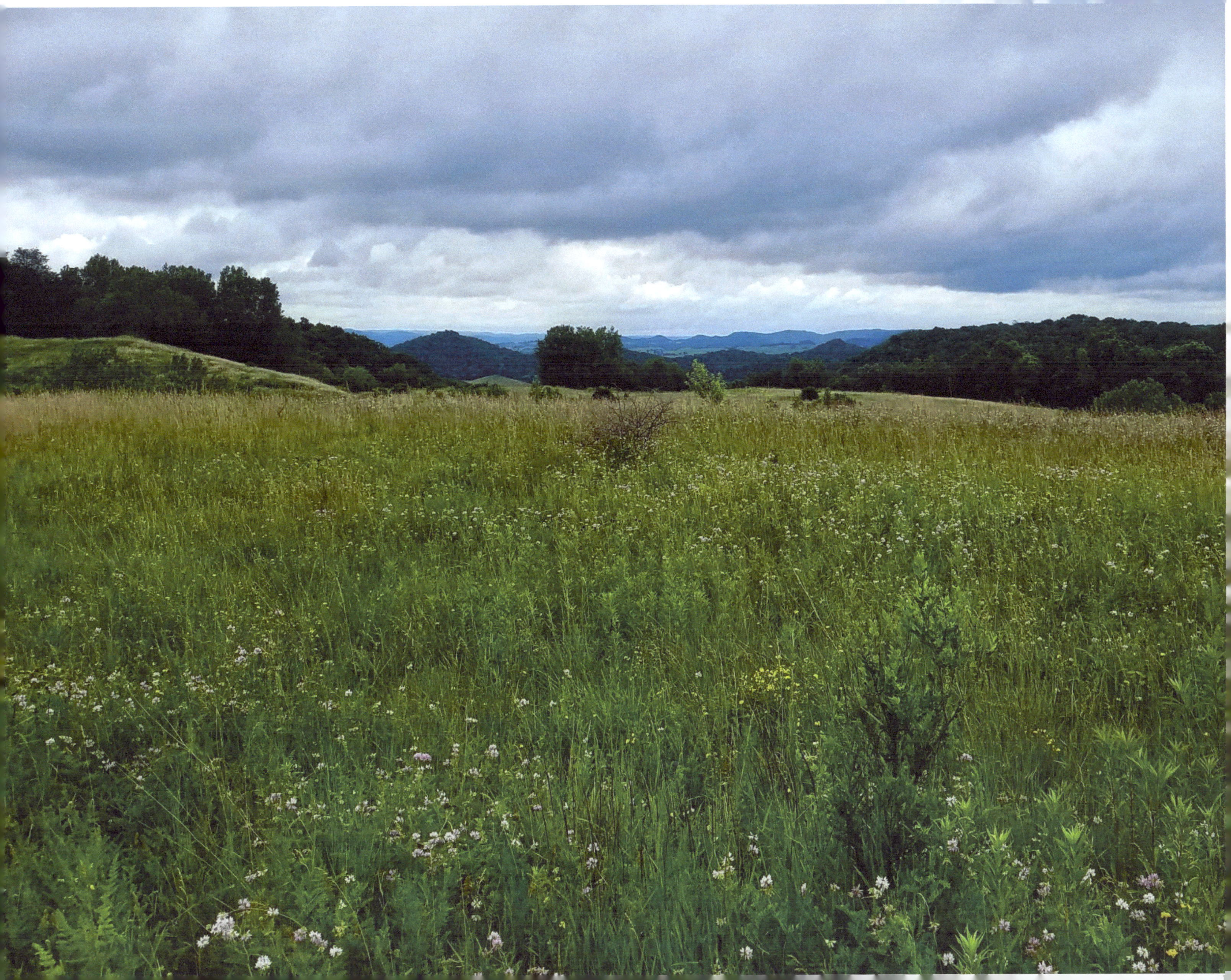

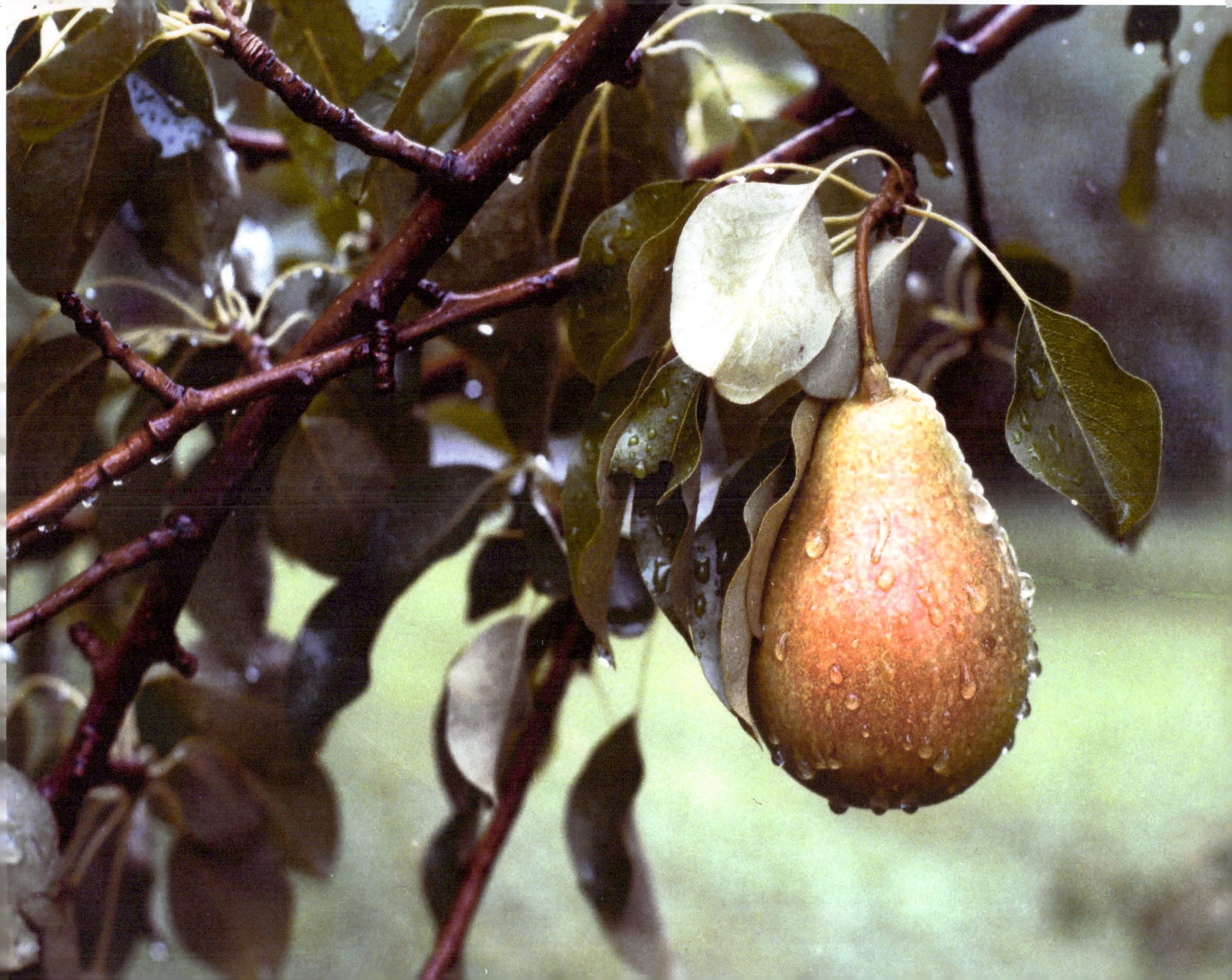

STAINED GLASS ORGINAL BY WILLIAM D. VAN ATTA JR.

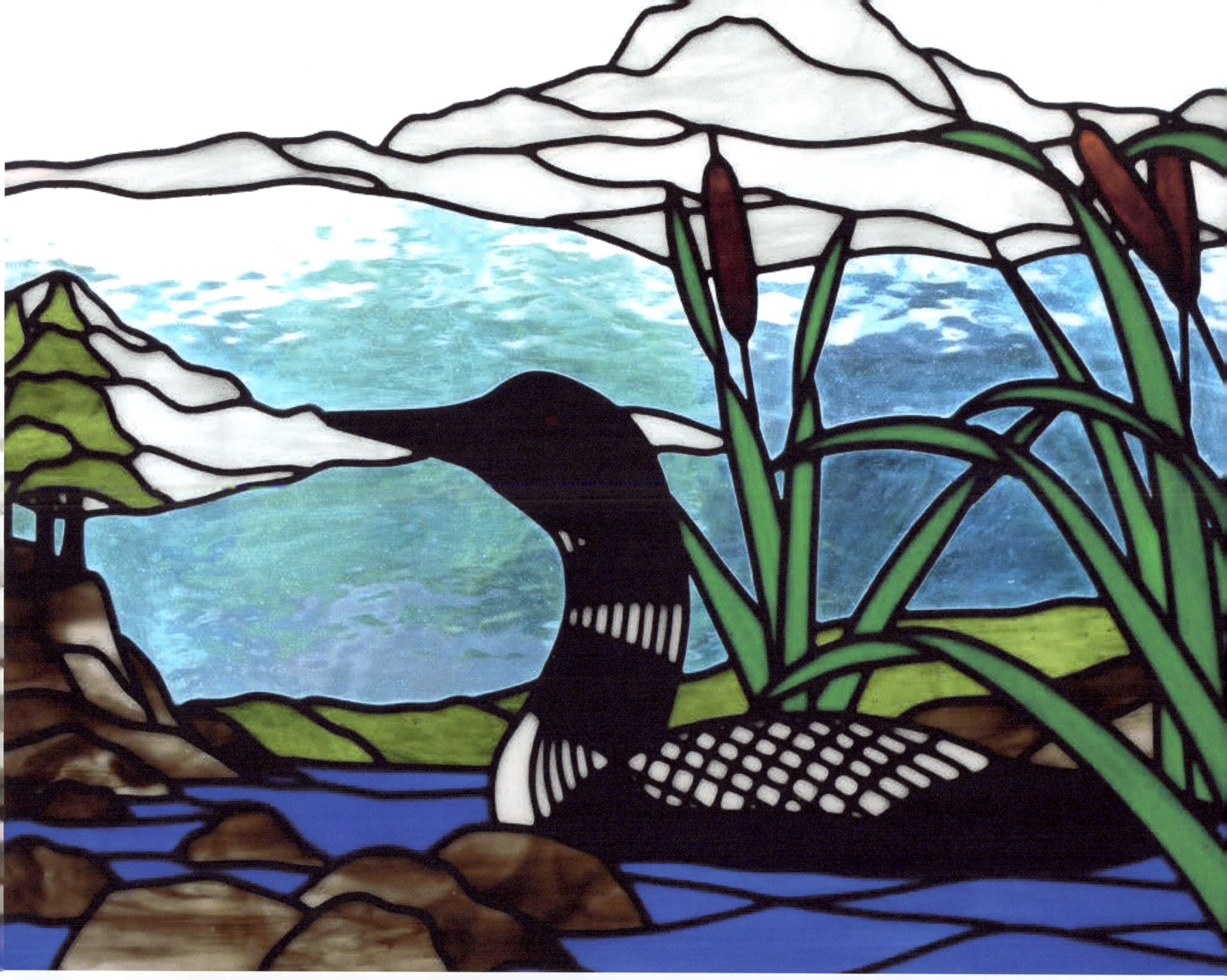

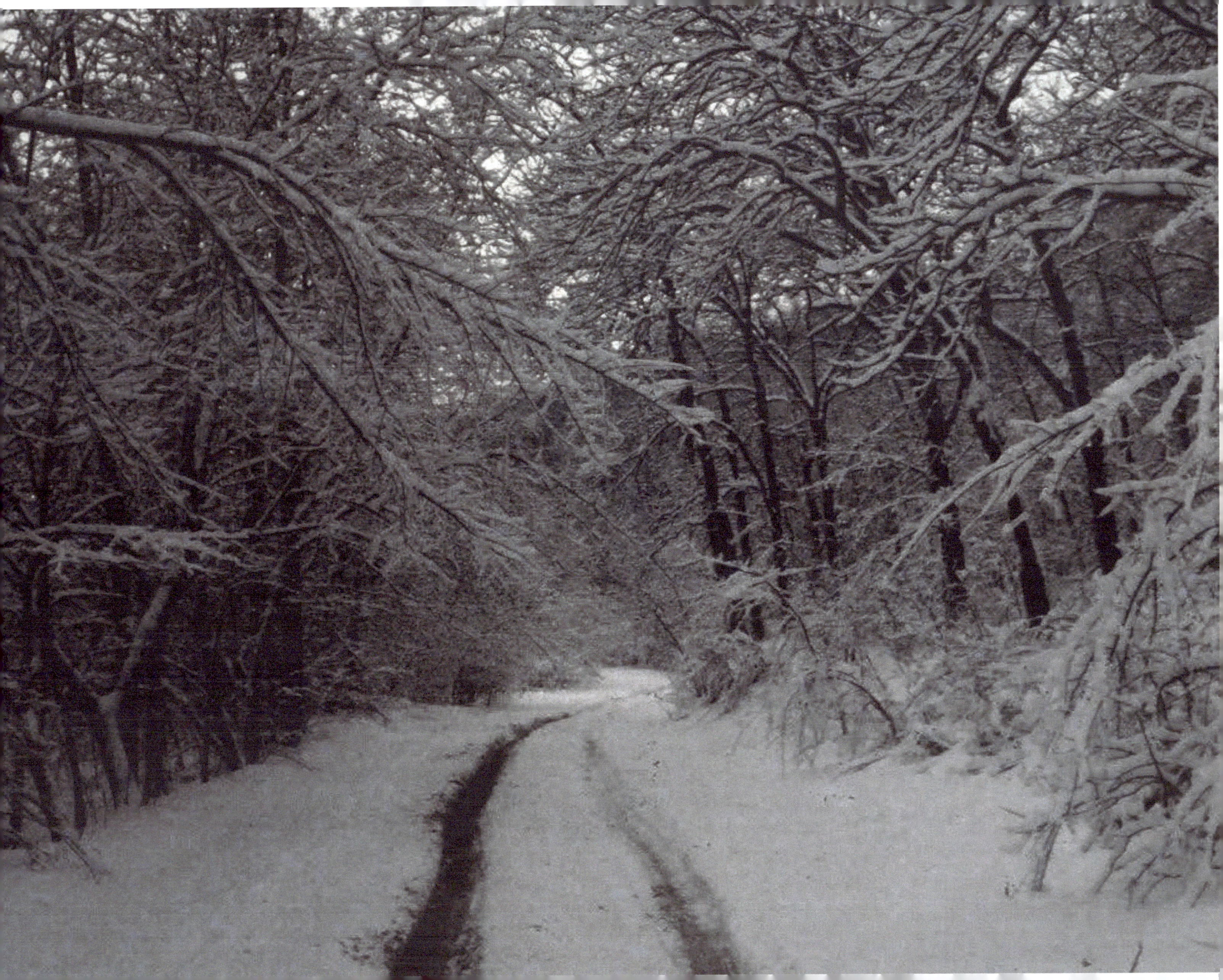

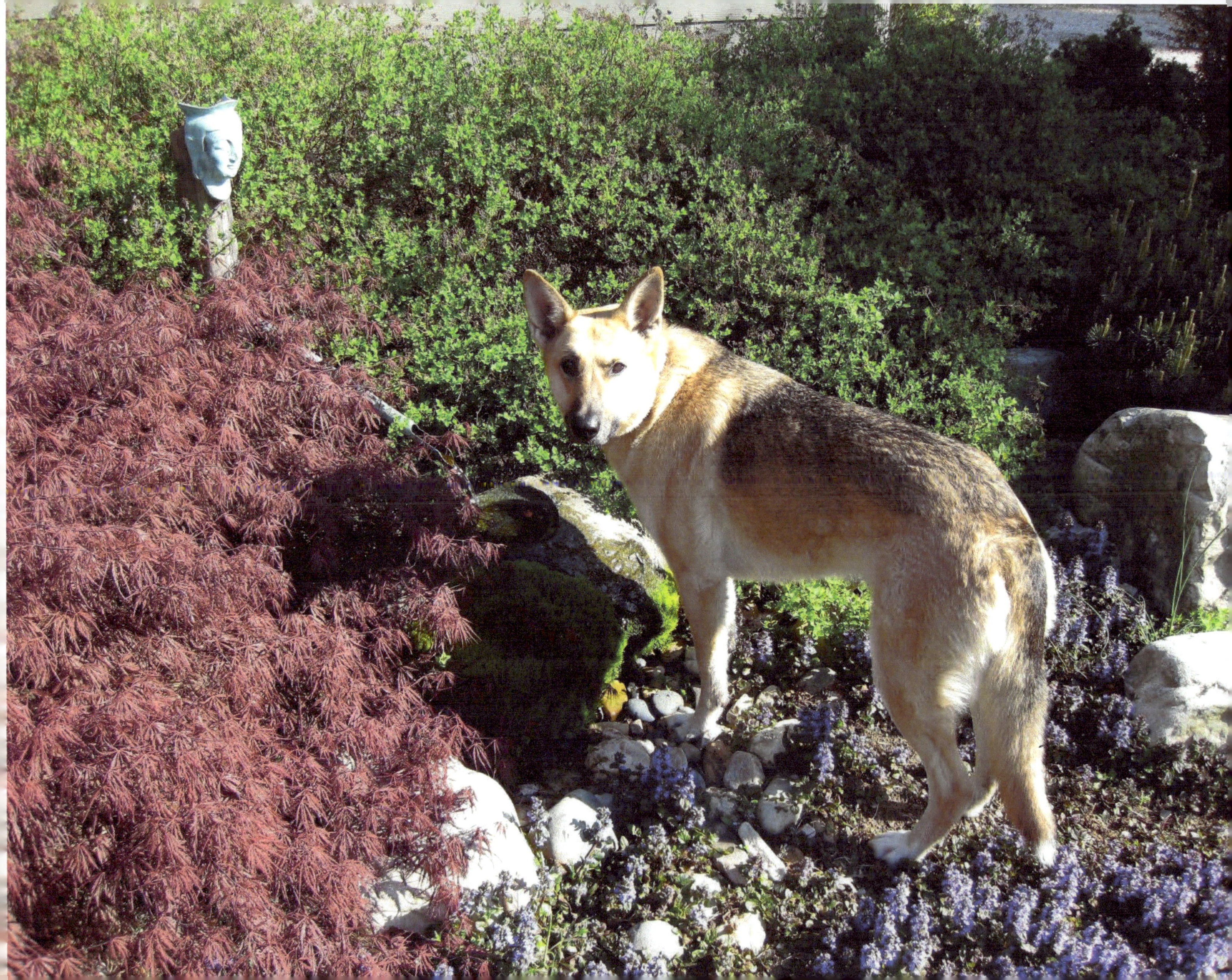

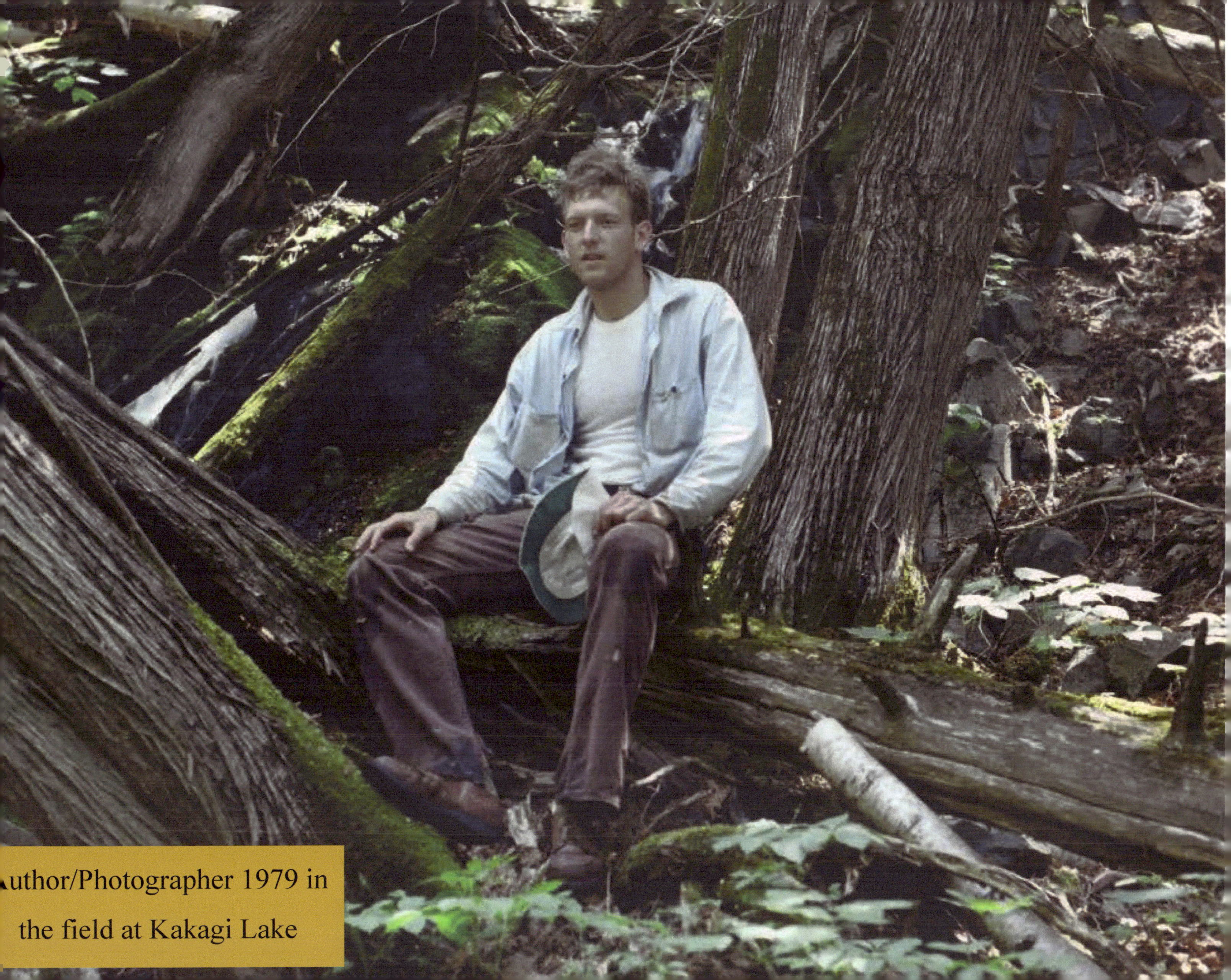

Author/Photographer 1979 in
the field at Kakagi Lake

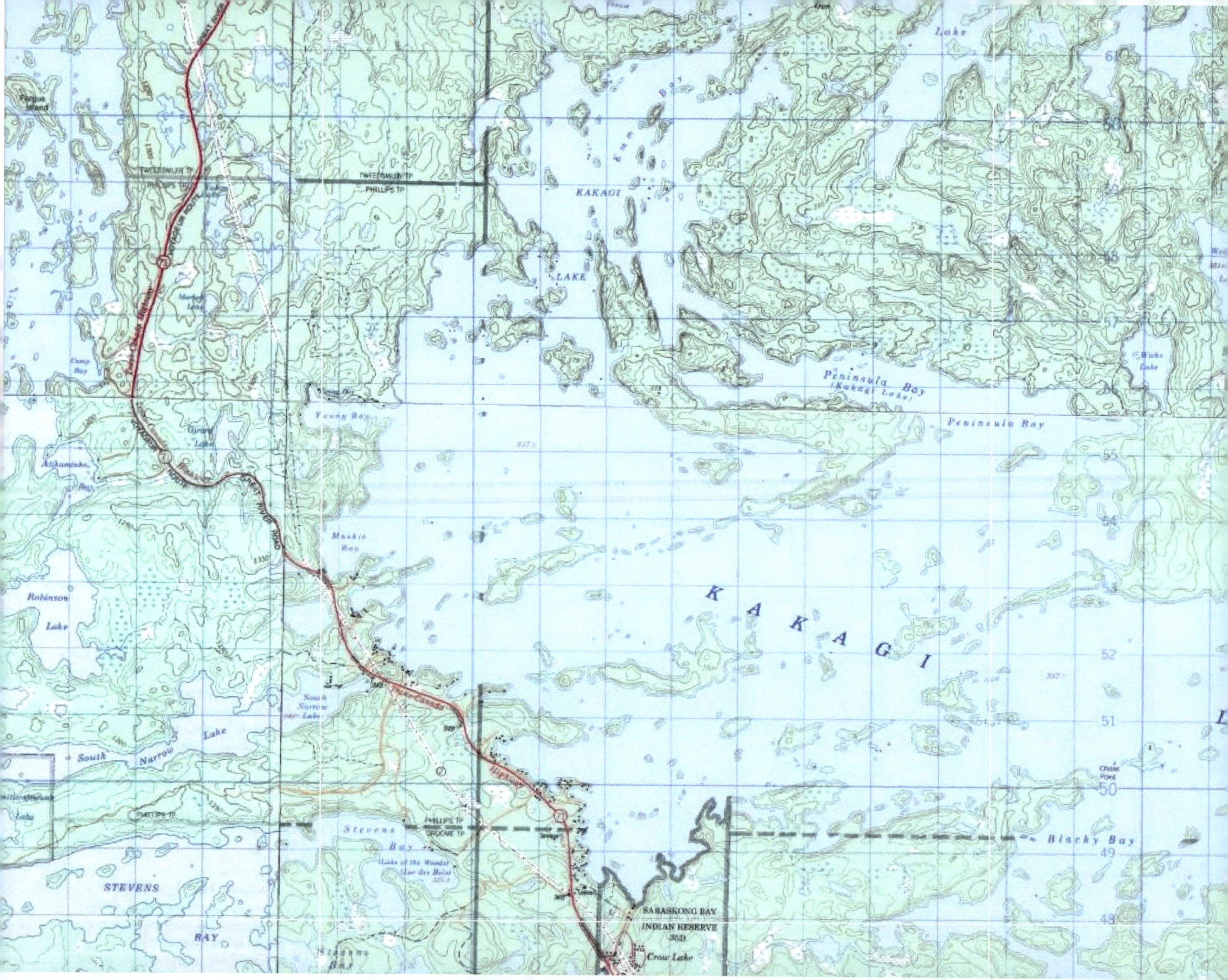

Fergus Island
TWEEDSMUIR TP
TWEEDSMUIR TP
PHILLIPS TP
KAKAGI
LAKE
Peninsula Bay
(Kakagi Lake)
Peninsula Bay
Wicks Lake
Camp Bay
Marshall Lake
Young Bay
Atikaminke Bay
Girard Lake
Muskie Bay
Robinson Lake
K A K A G I
South Narrows Lake
South Narrow Lake
PHILLIPS TP
Stevens Bay
PHILLIPS TP
GROOME TP
Lake of the Woods
(Lac des Bois)
STEVENS
BAY
Stevens Bay
Blacky Bay
Crane Point
SABASKONG BAY
INDIAN RESERVE
35D
Crow Lake

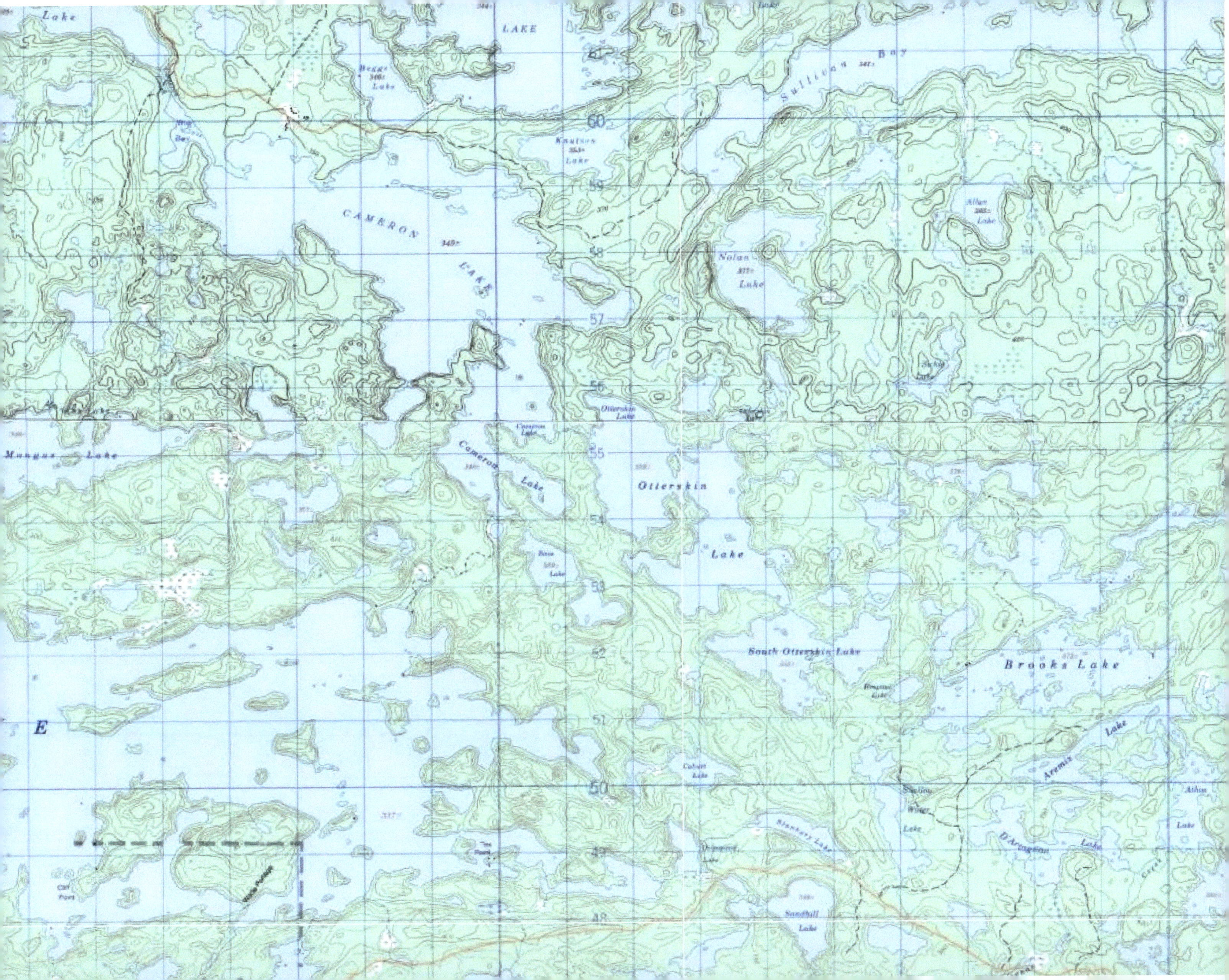

Lake
LAKE
Sullivan Bay
Beggs Lake
Knutson Lake
Albus Lake
CAMERON
Nolan Lake
LAKE
Jackin Lake
Otterskin Lake
Mungus Lake
Crespian Lake
Cameron
Lake
Otterskin
Lake
Bass Lake
South Otterskin Lake
Brooks Lake
Aremis Lake
Cobett Lake
Athus Lake
E
Stanbery Lake
Stellon River Lake
D'Arcagnan Lake
Creek
Deepwood Lake
Sandhill Lake
CBV Point

9 781917 399005